THE HOUR OF THE TIGER

Induk Pahk 박인덕

The Hour
of the Tiger

INDUK PAHK

AUTHOR OF *September Monkey*

 HARPER & ROW, PUBLISHERS

NEW YORK

IN MEMORIAM

TO

Dr. William F. Quillian, president
of Wesleyan College, Macon, Georgia,
who opened up a new world to me,
with affection and gratitude, I
dedicate this book

Contents

Preface

At long last "Berea in Korea," a self-help vocational school for boys, was founded on March 20, 1964, in Seoul, Korea.

How nicely it was put by a friend who knows me well, "There will come a day when she can say, 'I have arrived at my destination after traveling so far for so long.' "

To establish "Berea in Korea" has been my goal for thirty-five years. However, every moment of striving has been a challenge, and I find it most exciting and rewarding to conquer situations and vanquish the odds.

Finally, I have arrived at my destination and truly I can shout to all the world,

"Thank you, Heavenly Father, it's a reality—'Berea in Korea'!"

The content of this book tells of the years of struggle and setback before my dream was realized and also of the joys and rewards along the way.

It is my hope that you will find as much pleasure and

enrichment, as much strengthening of faith, in reading it as I have had in living it.

In *The Hour of the Tiger* I have tried to convey my heartfelt thanks to my thousands of friends in the United States and Canada who have made my lifetime dream of a "Berea in Korea" a living reality.

I also want to express my special appreciation to those who have given me such invaluable help with the manuscript itself —my lifelong friend Mrs. William F. Becker, who did so much in helping me set down the first draft, Edward R. Sammis, consulting editor to Harper & Row, and Susan Greenwald, editorial assistant, who helped me bring the manuscript into final form.

INDUK PAHK

1

*

Joy to the World

IT WAS THE EVENING of my eighth day on retreat. In the dusk of the small chapel I had been on my knees at the prayer rail for almost half an hour.

Like sentinels, two altar candles stood before me, tall and straight and white. Their pale flames flickered, casting long, wavering shadows. Through the open door came a light spring breeze, fragrant with the scent of myriad growing things, for this was mid-May, and all the flowers and shrubs, the magnolias, dogwood, and apple trees, were beginning to burst into bloom.

Within myself, I felt only a great weight. Silently I prayed that it might be lifted from me and that I might feel something of the tranquillity of my surroundings. I had reached a point where I could not go on much longer. Something had to happen.

Six months had passed since I received the greatest blow of my life. It was not so much the material loss as it was the betrayal by one in whom I had placed my trust that rankled.

Ever since then I could hardly say that I was alive. It would be more accurate to say that I existed. It was not so much a pain that I bore within me as a great emptiness—an emptiness that would not let me rest.

I knew the critical moment for me was not far away. That was why I was here. If I were ever to have a chance, it would be here, in this restful place of retreat.

I had been on my knees for the last seven nights in this quiet chapel. It had become my special haven.

But in this past week I felt nothing. I experienced nothing, no peace—not the release I was seeking—rather a mounting tension as time passed and I was given no sign. I knew well enough that if I did not find peace here, under these conditions, then I would never find it. I wanted to cry out, "Why, God, hast Thou forsaken me?"

My eyes followed the flickering candle flames. I concentrated all my faculties in a supreme effort to make contact with the Infinite as the only source from which I could draw my strength.

And then the spring breeze died away. The silence in the chapel grew intense. The pale yellow flames wavered no more, but stood straight up, as erect and straight as the candles themselves.

Into the silence fell a sound, the soft, deep chiming of a clock striking the hour of midnight—each note slow and separate and silver. And as the last note struck twelve, out of nowhere came the word—softly, softly, in the sleepy voice of a railroad conductor—"Kyoto! Kyoto!"

Another midnight, another critical moment in my life, far, far across the world and long ago. And I found the experience was still vivid in my mind.

I was traveling across Japan by train, before World War II, bound for Yokohama where I was to board a ship for America. I had just been through a difficult time. It was very fortunate for me that while I was going through this emotional upset, kind friends in the United States had made it possible for me to go there and start life anew. But I had not yet been able to put from me the burden of unhappy memories.

En route to Yokohama, I was half-dozing in the railway carriage when I heard the conductor call out, "Kyoto! Kyoto!"

Kyoto! It had always been a magic name to me. It is Japan's most beautiful city: the citadel of antiquity, a place of gnarled pines, formal gardens, and lovely temples. There is a Japanese saying that one works in Tokyo to be able to live in Kyoto.

I knew that we were scheduled to reach that city at midnight. The Japanese are so punctual in the running of their trains that when the conductor spoke the word "Kyoto," it was as if a clock had struck the hour.

I sat up in my seat. All around me people were sleeping. The conductor and I were the only moving figures in this shadow world. The train windows were dark. But beyond them, in my mind's eye, I could see this magical city.

The strangeness of it all—the half-light, the hour, the stirring of my imagination—had a mysterious effect on me. Kyoto! Midnight! The dividing point. The darkness of deep night had ended; the new day had just been born.

And so it was with my life. The past with its suffering was behind me. My new day had begun. Here, in this little chapel in western Massachusetts, once more I had the same feeling. Peace—and with it, strength—came to me.

I got to my feet and started up the stairs to bed. On a landing stood the clock, a lovely old Westminster grandfather clock, which had chimed the hour of midnight in such mellow tones.

An impulse came over me to speak to that clock as to a faithful friend. I paused on the landing, smiled, and said in my mind, "Thank you, Mr. Big Chime Clock. I am a changed person. I want you to be the first to know."

I went on up the stairs to my room. My bed was placed so that I would sleep facing the window. I undressed and went to bed, lying there for a moment looking out at the sky, so bright with stars.

Gently, almost without knowing it, I drifted off to sleep.

Some time later I was startled out of my slumber by the sound of a harsh, ugly voice. The voice was speaking to me, saying, "It cannot be done!"

Still not quite awake, I heard my own voice answering, "What? What can't be done?"

Again the voice spoke, still gratingly, "You cannot win your case! Your school will never be built!"

By this time my heart was beating so quickly and so loudly, that I felt I was about to suffocate. The same sensation I had known so often in recent months came over me once more, the sensation of sinking.

Then, holding my hand against my heart to quiet its beating, I sat up in bed, and called out in a firm, strong voice, "It can be done! It *will* be done!"

Up until the moment of my great blow, the pattern of my life from the very hour and place of my birth had appeared to be shaped in the direction of a single purpose.

I was born in the Hour of the Tiger, the Day of the Dragon and the Year of the Monkey. The village of my birthplace was situated halfway between the mountains—the Tiger's lair—and the sea—the domain of the Dragon.

The name of the village was Monyangtul, which means "remote place." In a way it was remote, for it was the last village to the west of the port of Chinnampo in North Korea, on an inlet of the Yellow Sea. But growing up there also gave me a sense of being a part of the world, for from the hill behind our house I could see the ships go by bound for far places: Mukden, Yokohama, Hong Kong, Singapore, and sometimes even San Francisco.

The village was a cluster of about twenty tan, mud-walled houses, thatched with yellow rice straw. All the people who lived there made their living by farming, walking out every day with their oxen to work on their land. In Korea, farmers prefer to live together in a single village, rather than in separate houses off by themselves as in America.

Since there was no other way to earn a livelihood except by farming, and my father had long ago decided to devote his life to being a scholar, my mother supported the family by going out every day to work on the farm.

Our farm had been in the family for a long time. It had belonged to my "inside grandfather," that is, my father's father. Since my father was his only son, my grandfather always had a splendid dream for him—that he should try for the greatest honor in the land, which was to take the Royal Examination. Whoever came out first in that examination would have a chance to become Prime Minister of Korea.

That was all my grandfather ever thought about—the day when my father would become Prime Minister. My grandfather was the kind of man who set his heart on one goal and then subordinated all else to it. In his view, it was Number One—or nothing.

This feeling was so strong in him that on the day my father was born he planted two trees, not very far apart, at the foot of the slope just beyond the end of his farm.

When his family inquired why he had planted the trees in that way, he told them they were for the acrobats.

"But why acrobats?" the family asked.

My grandfather did not hesitate in replying.

"On the day my son wins first place in the Royal Examination, then we will know that he is going to be Prime Minister. We will hold a big celebration here to honor the event. And the main feature of the celebration will be the acrobats who will perform on the tightrope stretched between those two trees."

My grandfather could have planted birch trees or larch which grow quickly, but it was also characteristic of him that the trees he planted were pine trees which take a long time to grow.

He said he chose pine trees because they remained green the year round and were therefore unchanging; also, they would grow strong and straight and tall. All these traits, he said, were the ones he expected his son to have, too. But even many years later when I went back to visit my home, I noticed that the two pine trees had scarcely yet grown tall enough to support a tightrope.

My father, who was a Confucian, spent every minute of the day poring over his books, or practicing his calligraphy, mastering the brush strokes to make the 250,000 characters of the Mandarin.

After many years he accomplished the first step in his projected career: He won first place in the provincial competition. At last he was eligible to compete in the Royal Examination which was held in the emperor's palace in Seoul, the capital of the country.

All this took place in the last days of the Yi Dynasty. A great flowering of Korean culture occurred under this dynasty which lasted for five hundred years. The most valued man was the scholar, who was often also both poet and artist. The primary purpose of the Royal Examination was to select the country's most outstanding scholar. The highest post in the land, short of being emperor (which was hereditary), was open to the one who triumphed.

The hopeful contenders were required to compose a poetic work, all on the same assigned topic, which was usually some aspect of Korea's natural beauties, such as a rock, a spring, autumn, a pine tree, or a waterfall. They were also judged on the skill and beauty of the brush strokes with which they rendered the Chinese characters.

All this took place before I was born. But my mother never tired of telling me of our scholars and the old traditions. She was so proud of my father. She loved especially to recount the story of how he went to take the Royal Examinations.

Three times he made his way on foot to and from the palace in Seoul where the examination was held. This was a distance of 150 miles. Three times he failed. How disappointed he must have been!

My mother told me, in the year I was born he was ready to go again—for the fourth time. But in that year the institution of the royal examination was abolished forever.

My father would never have another chance. But he did not sit around and brood. Not by any means. That was not my father's nature. There was no school in our village so the following year he started one. He gathered around him all the neighborhood children and all of those from villages nearby. Seated under a tree in the outer court of our home, he taught them how to write the beautiful Chinese characters and he passed on to them what he had learned of literature and philosophy. He had joy out of it, and satisfaction, too. I was too young to attend, but looked on from a distance.

My father used to say to me, "What a pity you are not a boy. Born in the Hour of the Tiger and on the Day of the Dragon! Such a rare and wonderful combination. What a shame it has to be wasted on a girl!"

I know now what was in his mind. Of course, I could never take the royal examination. But if only I had been a boy, I could have done something. Oh, yes, I could have done something!

My father had a great feeling for the pleasures of ordinary life. He loved his food and Korean wine. And he loved his tobacco, too. When I was six an epidemic of cholera swept the countryside and my father became very ill. I remember being in the room with him when he said,

"Bring me my tobacco. I want to feel the shreds with my fingers."

I went to get the tobacco but my aunt wouldn't let me back into the room, snatching the pouch from me and closing the door quickly. I couldn't understand why she kept me out. I hadn't done anything wrong. It was only later that I realized she did not want me to see my father die.

It was not until many years afterward that I got a glimpse of what a scholar's life must have meant to my father.

There was a certain courtyard in the palace in Seoul called the Secret Garden, which was private to the royal family and was only opened on the occasion of the examinations.

When I was grown and living in Seoul, I read in a newspaper one day that this garden was about to be opened to the public daily for the first time in history. All the stories my mother had told me about my father came back to me. I would go there at the first opportunity. I *must* go!

It was a lovely day in early spring when the chance finally came. Three or four friends went with me. We came up to the palace grounds. I was filled with anticipation. The heavy wooden gate, bound with iron bands, stood open.

What a feeling came over me as I first looked on that garden. It was just as my mother had described it, just as I had envisioned it for so many years. How I wished she could have seen that garden. A cloak of silence enveloped the courtyard. It was still with the stillness of the past—except for the gentle splashing of a fountain, with the water falling down, then running off into a little brook at one side.

The azaleas were in bloom, creating banks of flaming pink against the boulder-bordered paths, beneath the more delicate pink of the cherry trees.

Overhead, the boughs of weeping willows were bent in silent benediction. And all at once the Secret Garden was empty no more. In my mind's eye it was peopled with ghostly figures, so quiet, so solitary, so dignified; each in his white scholar's robe; each with his tall, narrow stovepipe hat, containing his long braids bound tight with a horsehair net.

Each of these phantoms carried in his hand his roll of rice paper, and in his *podari* (personal bundle) he had the soft, sharp-pointed Chinese brush and ink stone and ink cake for inscribing the Chinese characters.

And then—I could imagine that I saw my father! What a handsome man! So dignified, and at the same time so vibrant with life!

Only here, in this setting, on the scene of his testing, could I fully appreciate his achievement—the spirit, the determination he must have had to go through it all.

The examinations were always held about this time of year in the open garden outdoors. Here, on just such an afternoon, he had faced the ordeal.

He must have sat cross-legged with the other scholars and worked at top speed in total absorption. How great must have been the suspense, the tension. For at the end of those hours one came out of that secret garden either a hero—or a nobody (at least in my grandfather's view).

Three times my father had undergone that test—and three time he had failed. If the examinations had still been held he would have gone back again to try a fourth time—and a fifth. And I knew he must have wished that a son could take it after him.

But the Yi Dynasty came to an end with the outbreak of the Sino-Japanese conflict and the Royal Examination was no more.

Then I remembered a remark my father was said to have made on the day I was born,

"Ah, well, I expect a girl-child is better than no child at all."

I wished at this moment I could pluck at his sleeve, the

sleeve of the white scholar's robe, and call out to him,

"But Father! Do you have reason to be disappointed in me?
I have my B.A. degree from Wesleyan in Macon, Georgia,
and my M.A. from Columbia.

"It is true that I do not have my Ph.D. But I have published
a book, *September Monkey*. Even though I was not a boy,
have I then turned out so badly in your eyes?"

I seemed to feel my father's presence. I seemed to hear his
voice in the whispering of the wind in the willows.

Can those we love hear us, even though they are no longer
here? Sometimes I think so; the human yearning to reach them
is so powerful that I feel there must be some basis for belief.

It was only when I came to write this book that I realized
there was a channel, a direct line going on, in spite of disappointments, down through the generations.

I had one brother younger than myself. A month after my
father's death he, too, died. Now we were alone in the world,
my mother and I. Just the two of us, two women together.

My mother had lost everything that she valued—her husband and her son.

What did she have left? Not much—just me, little "September Monkey"—but, well, as my father had said, a girl was
better than nothing at all.

You see, in Korea, the aging father and mother are not sent
to an old age home; there are no such places. They are cared
for by their sons so long as they live. But what good is a
daughter? At that time in Korea there was no school nearby to
which a girl could be sent. (The first schools for girls had been
started by missionaries, but they were mostly in Seoul, far
from where we lived.) There was nothing for which a girl
could be trained. A girl was fit for marriage—nothing else.
And I was not even a very good prospect, since I had no
dowry.

The relatives appointed an heir to inherit the estate of my

father, according to custom. When the estate was settled, the oxen were gone, the rice fields were gone, our lovely house with its inner and outer compounds was gone. My mother was left with her share—the equivalent of about fifteen dollars—and a daughter on her hands to be reared.

But my mother did not sit in a corner and weep. She got busy at once.

My mother was a remarkable woman of indomitable character. Brought up a Buddhist and without formal education, she was naturally endowed with a kind of primal wisdom—something like a quality that you in the West call horse sense. All my days, when I found myself in strange places, in unfamiliar situations, some phrase of hers, some bit of philosophy, some fragment of her teaching, came forth to sustain me.

She was a handsome woman, too, of medium build but sturdy, always composed, yet at the same time dynamically energetic. She never made a movement unnecessarily, nor wasted any words. She was also very clever with her hands, doing, among other things, some beautiful weaving.

I inherited her physique, and I suppose it was because she fed me and cared for me so well in my early childhood that I have enjoyed the best of health myself under many conditions, thriving on a regime of hard work and strenuous schedules all my life.

At some point during the period of mourning we were visited by a distant cousin who had become a Christian. He spoke to my mother of the solace of God's mercy in times of sorrow.

My mother responded at once to the idea of a loving, caring, personal God, a concept she had not encountered in Buddhism, and to the way of love to be found in accepting Jesus Christ. Mother wanted to know where she could learn more about this beautiful new way, and my cousin told her.

In the port town of Chinnampo in North Korea, about three miles from our village, was a Methodist church. Mother made up her mind we would pay the church a visit.

I remember well the day we set out. It was biting cold; the wind howled with an eerie sound and blew the snow into drifts. Mother had bundled me up with a yellow padded jacket, trousers over my pink shirt, and little padded boots. (Mother still wore white as a sign of mourning.)

As we drew near the church, I could hear the sound of singing. It was Christmas Day; the congregation was singing, "Joy to the World!"

Ah, the indelibility of impressions when one is seven years old! The spirit! The lift! The joyousness! I always loved singing. My mother had a beautiful contralto voice. But I had never heard such a spontaneous outburst as from these massed, uplifted voices rolling out across the snow.

I did not know it was Christmas; I would not have known what Christmas was. There was no tree—there were no decorations of any kind—just the ringing voices and someone telling a story about the Child of Bethlehem.

How many, many happy Christmases I have enjoyed since then, with my own family, with my daughters and my grandchildren, or with friends and their children in places far away. But none of them has ever surpassed in vividness that first awed, bewildered, scarcely understood contact with the faith that was to sustain me throughout my life.

Mother and I went in. The church was built in the shape of an "L." The women sat along one branch of the "L," and the men along the other.

According to Confucian principles which governed Korean society at that time, males from the age of seven upward were not permitted to sit in the same room with females—and with the exception of relatives, they were not to have any contact with them whatever. The pulpit was placed in the angle so that the minister could speak to both the men and the women.

We listened to more hymns—and I loved them all. Then more speaking, and still more hymns.

At the end of the service, a woman greeted us with a smile and urged us to stay, explaining that gifts were about to be distributed to the children.

We children stood around in a circle, tongue-tied, waiting, our eyes wide with expectation. The presents were all the same: a pencil for each boy, handkerchiefs for all the girls. But when the dispenser of gifts came around to me, I was handed not a handkerchief but a pencil!

How amazing it is that a small event can influence the direction of one's life, just as a branch, fallen from above, can alter the course of a stream.

That pencil! It had a green eraser, I remember, and a big "No. 2" which meant it was not too hard and not too soft. How can people today, who have so much, feel what I felt at the sight of that pencil! It was yellow, the color of sunlight. The green at the tip symbolized spring, youth, hope—hope renewed, life everlasting. I turned it round and round in my hand. It was so straight, so smooth. And it was mine! Why— in all of our village, there was not another child, boy or girl, who owned a pencil! Unlike the other children, I had no father now. But I did have a pencil.

I looked at it in fascination. One of the missionaries said it came from a place called F. W. Woolworth's store, far, far across the sea. Somehow it stuck in my mind, so that years later—but I am getting ahead of my story. My pencil was blunt at the end, of course, and I could hardly wait for it to be sharpened.

My mother and I started across the snow, back to our village. I wanted to carry that pencil. But my mother would not let me have it. She knew I could so easily drop it in the snow, and then it would be gone forever.

In our village, there was an aging scholar who had been a friend of my father's. Mother sent for him to come and teach me the Korean alphabet. It is a phonetic alphabet, which has ten vowels and fourteen consonants—twenty-four letters in all—forming one hundred forty phonetic symbols.

I still remember the day the scholar appeared at our house. I could not take my eyes off his topknot, which he wore piled high on the top of his head and tightly bound in its horsehair net. This was the mark of an educated man.

Mother sharpened my yellow pencil with a kitchen knife and sat me down on the floor, which was heated by the pipes passing beneath it from our *ondol* stove. Mother watched me with a vigilant eye. She wasn't going to fool around wasting money on trying to teach me if I did not have the brains to learn (at that time in Korea brains were considered to be the exclusive property of the men).

My work with the alphabet must have satisfied her, for she appeared to have made up her mind then and there that I could be educated.

But since I was a girl, this decision of hers posed a problem. The only schools for girls in Korea had been started by the missionaries, and the nearest one was in the city of Pyongyang forty miles away.

Mother, not knowing what to do, went off by herself and prayed. For a solid week she prayed. King Solomon prayed for wisdom; Mother prayed for an idea.

Then an old, old story which she had heard as a child flashed into her mind, a story which had never been written down.

It concerned a Chinese girl in the misty past who had a burning desire to become a general. She did her hair like a boy, dressed as a boy, and became a line soldier. She rose through the ranks to become a general as she had dreamed, and no one knew her secret.

Then she fell in love with another general, was forced to reveal herself, and finally married her counterpart, to live happily ever after.

In this story Mother found her idea. She would disguise me as a boy and send me to a boy's school.

Not far away in the village of Dukdong there was such a school where a distant cousin was headmaster. Mother schemed with our cousin so that I could enter there. She rented a room next to the school so that I could go home any time I wanted to.

It was easy enough to change my name from the feminine *Imduk* to the masculine *Induk,* the name which I have kept.

I stayed in school at Dukdong for a year. I must say I got great enjoyment out of being a boy. I reveled in the freedom, in hunting for birds' eggs, making whistles, and flying kites.

Mother seemed very pleased with me, too. In the village markets she sold enough of her weaving to buy some odds and ends, tied them up in her pack and set out on foot to make her living as a peddler. It has sometimes occurred to me that in a sense I followed in my mother's footsteps. I too sell notions— only notions of a different sort.

It was not until many years later, when I began writing my second book, in fact, that a friend pointed out to me the following thought:

Was it because I had pretended to be a boy in a boys' school that the suggestion of my founding a "Berea in Korea" for boys fell on such fertile ground when it was first made to me? Was it all a part of some extraordinary plan for my life? If so, I had carried my inspiration all these years in my subconscious.

One of my strong motivating forces has always been to help the women of Korea. Although my school experience served as a signpost toward helping the boys of Korea, I later realized that in educating the boys, I was indirectly bringing about a better life for the women of my land, also. For thousands of years the women as well as the men of Korea had been forced to spend long hours at heavy farm labor on a small plot of ground because of the old-fashioned farming procedures. I wanted to work toward the day when wives and daughters would be freed from these tasks for a richer and more rewarding life.

I had just finished my first year at Dukdong when Mother learned of a new school for girls which a Methodist missionary had just started at Chinnampo. She decided to enroll me there. I was able to live at the school while Mother, making her base at the house of my uncle, slung her peddler's pack over her shoulders and took to the road again to earn my tuition. It must have been a hard life. But Mother seemed happy enough to make this sacrifice in order to see that I got educated.

The ocean had always fascinated me from the time I was a small child. Our village was three miles from the port of Chinnampo. It was on high ground. From a nearby hill, I could see the Yellow Sea with the plumes of smoke rising from the ships in the distance.

I used to lie on my back among the daisies and say to myself,

"What's beyond the clouds? What's beyond the mountains? What's beyond the sea? Someday—someday I shall go and find out."

The school which I attended now was also on a hill, and quite near the water. I could see the ships with their unfamiliar flags bound for nameless ports up north—or headed east for Japan, or for San Francisco, an unimaginable distance away on the other side of the sea.

More strongly than ever the desire to travel was implanted in my imagination—to go there, to see it all for myself someday.

The school was new and there were twenty girls, only two of us in the first class, my dear friend Simsung Yun and myself. Perhaps this affected my life, for when it came time to graduate we both had to make talks.

The teacher gave me the topic, "From the seed of suffering springs joy." I am certain now that she assigned this for my benefit, because she knew full well how hard my mother had to work to keep me in school for four years, and also how very, very poor I was.

I must pause and pay tribute to my teacher, my first teacher of speech. Like my mother she was energetic, but unlike my mother, she was very austere. When she said, "Do this," you did it. There were no two ways about it.

First she rehearsed us in the classroom after hours. Then she took us up to the church on top of the hill.

The years have not dimmed the memory of her square-shouldered figure, topped by her broad face with its flashing eyes, as she roared at me like a major general:

"Chin up! Don't droop. Do you want to drop your words on the floor?

"Don't mumble! Why do you bother to speak at all if you can't make people understand what you say? Pronounce every syllable clearly so that I can understand. There—that's better."

The day came for graduation. We must have looked rather forlorn—just the two of us in our white graduation dresses between the pots of red azaleas on the huge platform in the church, before an audience of two hundred.

But I must have done fairly well for the applause was enthusiastic. In the audience I caught a glimpse of my mother's face, wearing a proud look. That was enough for me.

When I was twelve years old, the girl who was my fellow classmate announced that she was going to Ewha in Seoul and invited me to go along.

I was terribly excited by the idea of going to the big city far down south.

Simsung Yun with her father, and my mother and I, walked

the forty miles to Pyongyang, the largest city in the north, for no train passed through our village. The Mukden Express came roaring into Pyongyang with its big steam engine breathing smoke and fire. This time instead of watching it roar away bound for strange and mysterious destinations, my classmate and I climbed aboard. We were going to see for ourselves. What a great moment that was!

Mother came to wave good-by. She stood there on the platform absolutely dry-eyed, smiling, and full of instructions. I did not think anything about it at the time. I was too excited over the idea of going to Seoul.

It was only in later years, when I had to take leave of my own daughters, that I understood how she must have felt. I was her only chick—all she had in the world—and she let me go, leaving her all alone, without showing any emotion.

Mother gave me a dollar and fifty cents, saying it was her tithe, or 10 per cent of her estate. Sixty cents went for the ticket, and I had ninety cents left. I murmured something to the effect that I hoped my education wouldn't be too hard for her. Whereupon Mother replied, "I have no trouble with difficulties. Difficulties only have trouble with me."

It did not bother me in the least that the school had never been told I was coming.

Night had fallen by the time my classmate and I reached Ewha High School. My companion had a room ready for her. I tagged along. Everyone at the school seemed to assume that arrangements had been made for me also.

Promptly at ten o'clock, the light in the ceiling went out, turned off by a master switch in the office. We were plunged into darkness. I would have been frightened if my curiosity had not been aroused by this phenomenon.

I had never seen anything like this before—a light that could be turned on and off from somewhere else. I had known only the flickering oil lamps of the villages. My friend explained that this was something called an electric light. Then she went on to tell me that this lamp had been invented by a man in far-off America, who had also invented the talking machine. His name was Thomas Edison.

For some reason her story caught my imagination. Right then and there I made up my mind that I would cross the ocean and go see the country where such marvelous things were invented. Although at that time there seemed little chance of making my wish come true, the thought was never very far from my mind.

The next morning the principal called me to her office. As I stood before her desk, she asked me, "Do you have anyone to pay for your room and board?"

"Isn't this school free?" I asked.

"The tuition is, but your lodgings will cost one dollar and fifty cents."

"Well, that's all right," I said proudly, holding out my hand. "I have ninety cents."

"But you need sixty more cents to stay just for one month. Can you make up the balance?"

"Of course I can. Let me work for you. I can certainly work one dollar and fifty cents' worth a month."

The principal looked skeptical and I could tell she was ready to refuse. In my desperation I rudely burst out, "I want to go to school! I have to go to school! I'll study hard and I can take care of myself. I won't bother anyone."

In the end I was allowed to stay and after a while the principal and I became good friends. Some time later she said to me with a smile,

"Induk, do you remember the interview we had that first morning in my office? Well, you didn't know it, but that was when you passed your entrance examination."

My teacher at the elementary school, who had drilled into me the rules of good public speaking, would have been proud

of me for I was chosen to give the Christmas message to the
school that year. Already my career was being shaped. As I
look back on it, I think God was preparing me for the
work He wanted me to do.

During my beginning year at Ewha High School, I was put
in contact with my first friend in America. All I knew about
him in the beginning was that he was blind, and upon the
recommendation of the school, he was willing to help me gain
an education. It was thanks to his generosity that I was able
not only to continue three years at Ewha, but to go on for four
more years at Ewha College.

Years were to pass before I was to meet my sponsor in
person; it was a moving moment for me as I shall describe
later on. But in the meantime I suppose my desire to answer
his letters and to keep up a correspondence with him proved
my greatest spur to learning English.

What a thrill it was for me when I received my first communication from him. His letter was typewritten, single-
spaced, and three pages long. I had to take it to the principal
to ask her to translate it for me. He wrote that I brought a new
interest into his life and that he prayed we would meet someday. ". . . I hope that you will study hard," he said, "the
whole world lies ahead of you."

In one letter he had managed to establish a deep personal
relationship. I never ceased to feel grateful to him. In attempt-
ing to do what I could to repay his generosity, I obtained
scholarships for sixty boys and girls in Korea, and working-aid
scholarships for thirty-one Korean men and women to come to
the United States.

I graduated from Ewha in due time, first in my class. Then,
for a number of years, I taught in the schools of Seoul. During
this period I married a football player and had my two daughters, Iris and Lotus.

I was twenty-eight years old when the opportunity arose for

me to enter the United States to continue my education. A missionary friend of mine got a scholarship for me from Wesleyan College in Macon, Georgia, through Dr. William F. Quillian, who was then president of the college.

No chance like it would ever come again. But I would have to leave my two darling little girls behind. It was the hardest decision I had ever been forced to make.

My marriage had not worked out, for my husband preferred the old ways and I was committed to the new. But my husband's mother, "Inside Grandma," had begged to be allowed to care for Iris and Lotus, and continually urged me to take advantage of the opportunity.

My husband was alive, but I had the sole responsibility of educating my daughters. By accepting this opportunity for advanced study in America, I knew that in the long run I would be able to do much more for them.

My mother's strength of character and her courage, more than anything else, sustained me during this difficult time.

The moment came to say good-by to my mother and to my two little girls. The tears stung my eyes. I remembered what my mother said to me, so firmly, when I told her of my decision to go.

"If it's going to make you cry, then you shouldn't go. If you know you must go, then you shouldn't cry."

How many times in later years when my emotions threatened to give way under stress, have I heard my mother's strong voice saying, "Induk, whatever it is, if it's going to make you cry, don't do it."

2

✳

The Sowing of a Seed

THE VOYAGE across the Pacific took three weeks—
two weeks to Honolulu, one week to San Francisco. I used to
stand on the afterdeck and look out across the broad Pacific toward the land that I had left. I was sailing on one of
those ships I had seen as a little girl bound for far places. The
wonder of it never ceased to thrill me.

I had three immediate impressions of the United States—
space, plenty, and freedom.

It was such a vast country!

My scholarship was for Wesleyan College in Macon,
Georgia, the oldest chartered female college in the world. To
reach it, I crossed the continent by train. The landscape
seemed endless. Having never been out of Korea, I found it
hard to believe that one country encompassed so much territory within its borders.

Everywhere there was plenty. No one seemed to lack for
anything. What a striking contrast from my native Korea,
where so many people were so poor.

30

Then the freedom. The freedom politically—the freedom between the sexes. Boys and girls seemed to be utterly carefree, strolling arm in arm, hand in hand. Such a thing would be forbidden in Korea, according to old Confucian principles.

I had grown up under a double yoke: the yoke of the Japanese domination and the yoke of conformity to the old Korean way of doing things. For this reason, the freedom that I saw everywhere made the most profound impression on me.

Freedom was like the electric light which I had seen for the first time in Ewha School. If you had grown up with freedom, as you had grown up with the electric light, then you were inclined to take it for granted.

For me, the suddenness of my discovery made it all the more tremendous. I couldn't get enough of it.

At the same time I did not feel that I had the right to enjoy this freedom for myself unless I was also doing something to help the women at home—those who were not so privileged as I—to improve their lot. This was going to be a big undertaking; certainly it would not be fully realized within my lifetime or, perhaps, for many years beyond.

Why, it would take nothing less than a revolution to accomplish the change I envisioned for Korea. But why not? Why not? In America with its freedom, its resources, its energy, with a sparkle in the very air, if I couldn't accomplish something I would have nobody to blame but myself.

I arrived at Wesleyan on a Friday. On the following Sunday I had my first speaking engagement at the Rosser Bible Class of the Mulberry Street Methodist Church.

My study course was uneventful enough. I majored in philosophy and minored in sociology. In two years I would be able to qualify for a B.A. degree. But my chief extracurricular activity there was public speaking.

In the last days of the year 1927 the Quadrennial Convention of the Student Volunteer Movement was held at the huge white Masonic Auditorium in Detroit. I was invited to go as a representative from Wesleyan College. More than three thousand delegates had gathered there from all over the world.

The concluding day of the convention fell on New Year's Day, 1928. At about eleven o'clock the evening before, I had found a note in my hotel room telling me that I was one of three speakers who had been chosen to give testimonial messages at the closing session. One was to represent Africa, one the Near East, and I was selected to speak for the Far East.

I was absolutely dumfounded. I had no advance warning, no opprotunity to prepare anything. I could not understand why they had chosen me. Later, I found out that because China and Japan were antagonistic to each other, a representative from either country would have caused difficulties. On the other hand, who could object to a woman from the little country of Korea? What could be more harmless!

The morning of the closing session came. At exactly 10:45 I walked out on the platform. It seemed so wide and the auditorium seemed so enormous. In contrast, I felt so small. And indeed I was. At that time I weighed only one hundred and five pounds. A man came out from somewhere and lowered the microphone for me, so it would be easier for me to speak into it. I was conscious mainly of that section of stenographers, sitting with their pencils poised waiting to take down every word I said.

I had picked as my topic, "What Christianity has meant to me."

When I faced that audience, I had butterflies in my stomach. My knees were knocking together. Fortunately at that time skirts were quite long and I whispered to myself,

"Thank you, skirt, for hiding my knees so people cannot see how they are shaking."

I have never stood up to speak before a large audience without suffering from stage fright. I have since learned that stage fright is necessary—it keeps you on your toes. It happens to anyone who is worth his salt. But I didn't know it at that time.

My mind groped for some opening words. I have learned that the first statement is all-important. It must be strong. You must capture the attention of your audience. Then, you must continue to hold their interest.

I choose words which are active, not passive. Then I look for a reference which is either completely local or very remote and strange. Anything in between is lukewarm.

Before I am to speak in a certain town or city I make it a point to brief myself. If I am going to speak in Hutchinson, Kansas, for instance, I try to find out everything I can about their salt mines.

At the other end of the spectrum I attempt to think of something that would be farthest from their experience, the stranger and more unfamiliar, the better. It was this end of the spectrum which I relied on now. With a big smile on my face, I said into the microphone:

"Sahae boke manhe badusipsio."

Then I added, "Which means in Korean, 'I wish that this year in particular will bring you many blessings.' "

I was so terrified at the time that after all these years I can still remember my opening statement. This is what I said:

"In the eighteenth and nineteenth centuries there have been many marvelous scientific discoveries which promise to alter the course of human history.

"But within our own time there has taken place the most marvelous discovery of all. I refer to the discovery of womanhood in the East.

"In my country, Korea, within my lifetime, I have seen schools for women develop for the first time in four thousand years. It is because of that school that I was educated, and because of that education I am able to stand here before you this morning.

"We are embarking upon nothing less than a revolutionary change in the patterns of family living. It will take Korean women many years to bring this into being. I may not live to see it happen, but believe me, it *will* happen."

Then I went on to tell how my mother had become a Christian; how she sent me to a boys' school; how women made their first great strides when the independence movement came and we took our place side by side with the men. I ended by paying homage to Jesus Christ who had made it all possible through the consecration of the missionaries.

During my short speech, I received four spontaneous bursts of applause. I had been scheduled to speak for fifteen minutes, but I said everything I had to say in eleven minutes.

I sat down with the hand clapping ringing in my ears. I was so excited I could hardly utter a word when people came up to me with congratulations. I thrilled again and again to hear what they had to say.

It was not until some months afterward that the incident occurred that was to give my life its purpose. But I think I may say that my career as a public speaker began that morning on that platform.

This was the first time I had ever stood before so large an audience and felt the words come when I needed them, felt the electric thrill of communication between those three thousand people of all continents of the earth and myself.

I knew now my life's work was to be in the service of God, who, in His own way, had made all this possible for me.

Right after I graduated from Wesleyan, I joined the Student Volunteer Movement and my travels, stumping for the Lord, began.

The S.V.M., as it was known, was an interdenominational group of students in colleges and universities who were interested in foreign missions. I was the first Oriental traveling secretary of the S.V.M. speaking in colleges and universities throughout the United States and Canada in behalf of the foreign missions.

I found this life very much to my liking. I am a restless soul—the tiger is always on the prowl, you know—and I enjoyed the experience of meeting new people and seeing new places.

I continued speaking before smaller groups—colleges, universities, church groups, clubs—all over the United States and Canada.

It was the start of a career during which I was to travel one and a quarter million miles by all forms of transportation, but mostly by the faithful Greyhound bus—without ever missing one single speaking engagement.

That spring I registered at the summer school of Columbia University to begin work on my master's degree, majoring in speech and in religious education. At Wesleyan, besides majoring in philosophy, I had also studied psychology and sociology, subjects which were to prove of use to me later in my lecturing.

Shortly before Thanksgiving of that same year I was asked to speak at Berea College in Berea, Kentucky. The invitation came about through my friend, Miss Hattie E. Stowe, sister of Leland Stowe, the well-known foreign correspondent; and this speaking engagement proved to be the turning point of my life.

As soon as I got off the bus in Berea, I felt right at home. It was a mild and beautiful autumn day; the fall is gentler in Kentucky than in the more northern parts of the country.

In the distance were the blue and hazy mountains, reminding me of our mountains in Korea. Around the college itself were gently rolling hills, also like those in Korea. The only difference is that we do not have Kentucky's famous bluegrass.

On my way to the auditorium where I was to speak I met

students hurrying from one class to another. Immediately I noticed something unusual about them. By this time I had spoken at many colleges and universities around the country, but these young people were unlike any others I had seen. They had an air about them that set them apart. Perhaps it was the expression in their eyes, or something about the way they carried themselves that bespoke an earnestness, a sense of purpose.

A few minutes later Dr. William J. Hutchins, who was then president of Berea, received me in his office. Dr. Hutchins was a distinguished educator, as were his two sons. One son, Robert M. Hutchins, became chancellor of the University of Chicago and is now with the Ford Foundation. The other, Francis S. Hutchins, was later to follow in his father's footsteps as president of Berea.

Berea was founded in 1855 when the antislavery movement was at fever-pitch, and the clouds of the Civil War were gathering on the horizon. A native Kentuckian named John C. Fee, an ordained minister and a determined abolitionist, built a home and a one-room school—which was also used as a church on Sundays—on one of the first foothills of the Blue Ridge Mountains. He named the school Berea after the town mentioned in the Bible, in Acts 17:10. The men of the Biblical Berea were distinguished for being open-minded.

The first teachers were recruited from Oberlin College in Ohio, which was anti-slavery, anti-caste, anti-rum, and anti-sin.

Three years later, Berea took a long stride forward when an Oberlin graduate came to Berea with the plan of turning the school into a college to be open to men and women alike, regardless of class, color, or creed. It would be a college which would provide the best possible education at the lowest possible cost.

From that day forward, Berea offered educational opportunities for the needy and the deserving; it has never departed from the principles and the philosophy of its founders.

In the early years the college department accounted for no more than one-tenth of the total enrollment. Now the pendulum has swung the other way. While a high school is still maintained, 90 per cent of the students today are enrolled in the college.

Also in the early years, the school charged a nominal tuition fee. But by 1892, when Berea's financial situation was no longer so precarious, and a practical labor program had been firmly established, it became possible for youngsters to work for their keep, and the tuition fee was abolished altogether.

Today Berea's work-study program affords some sixteen hundred students, who might otherwise be deprived of it, the chance to get a college education. They include both Negro and white students, many of whom come from isolated mountain areas. Also on the roster are about fifty foreign students.

All students must share in the school's labor program, i.e., contribute up to ten hours of work a week in one or more of the sixty-three organized departments on the payroll schedule. Among them are printing, farming, fireside industries, weaving, and brickmaking, as well as a bakery and candy kitchen.

Students can also work while they receive professional training in the hospital, in the laboratories, in the library, and on the poultry farm, where the most up-to-date equipment is provided.

Dr. Hutchins led me to the auditorium where the students were waiting for me. For a moment I suffered the familiar stage fright. Then I mastered it.

I spoke of my school days, when I masqueraded as a boy.| I told them how I had come to like boys' trousers better than those which we wore as girls, because the latter were held up with a sash, wound so tight under the arms that it was hard to breathe. The boy's belt, worn loose around the waist, was much more to my liking. I also told the story of my first experience at Sunday School and how I was given my No. 2 yellow pencil which had come from F. W. Woolworth's store across the sea.

By the time I had arrived at the account of my hard days in prison under the Japanese because of the part I played in the Korean independence movement, I had the audience with me. They were completely absorbed.

I sat down with the heady sound of spontaneous applause ringing in my ears. What a wonderful place Berea was! I could feel its pioneer spirit!

We have a saying in Korea:

"What you feel, you radiate." Now I knew what had struck me about these youngsters. They were radiating pride—pride and gratitude. They realized how fortunate they were to be there, because Berea at that time was not very large—with perhaps five hundred students. Having the chance to pay for their own education made them proud. They were grateful for the opportunity to be going to college.

This, I thought to myself, is the rounded education. Here is preparation for a complete life, with training for the hands as well as for the head.

Then, sitting there on the platform listening to Dr. Hutchins' closing remarks, pictures of Korean boys came into my mind, boys from country much like this. I remembered the young men I had seen in the villages. They were alert and intelligent, but without any chance of being educated. They were therefore doomed to walk after the oxen in the furrow, without rest, without hope of anything different—just like their fathers and their grandfathers before them, back to the beginning of time.

I remembered also the young men as I had seen them at the market place in Seoul, standing patiently and stolidly in line waiting for work—waiting day after day. I remembered them with their baggy pants padded against the cold, layer upon layer of patches. Each had his A-frame or his *giggy*, as it was called, strapped to his back. On this A-frame he could carry more than one hundred pounds. This conveyor is unique to Korea. It was his only implement, just as the untouchable of India has as his only implement, the broom. And with this he expects confidently to compete with the machine.

But most of all I remembered the expressions on their faces toward the end of a long day when they still had no work— after they had walked heaven knows how many miles from their villages just to get there. They were still hoping, still cheerful, still waiting to be called—knowing in their hearts they would be lucky if they could earn enough to buy a handful of millet for their families. Every time I saw them I made firm resolve: Someday in some way I would try to do something to help them.

Berea, I reflected, offered exactly the kind of education my countrymen needed. The Jewish people have a saying, "He who teaches not his son a trade, teaches him to steal."

I recalled from my readings in the Bible that nearly everyone had a trade. Paul was a tentmaker; Jesus was a carpenter.

The meeting broke up. Dr. Hutchins rose and stood towering at my side, smiling down at me. He was a kindly man, but there was a stern look about him, too—a quality that reminded me of my mother and filled me with awe.

Suddenly everything I had been thinking came pouring out of me. He listened attentively and sympathetically. Then he spoke the words that were to alter the course of my life forever.

I remember the moment well. Dr. Hutchins had taken my arm to help me down the short stairway to the auditorium floor. He was letting me go first. This in itself was an unusual experience, for in Korea it is always the man who goes first.

We have a parable in our country which vividly illustrates

what is considered to be the place of woman in our society.

It seems that a husband was out attending to his business one evening when a caller came to the door.

The housewife answered.

The caller inquired if the husband were home.

"I'm sorry," the housewife replied quite seriously, "there's nobody here."

And here I was not only going first, but I was the center of attention.

We had reached the auditorium floor.

"Why don't you," said Dr. Hutchins, "start such a school? Why not call it 'Berea in Korea'?"

"Berea in Korea"!

What a memorable phrase! What an exciting thought!

My head was full of stars. Oh, if ever I could achieve anything like that, my coming to the United States and leaving my daughters would be justified. My life would be rich and full.

Then I came back to earth as though I were being doused with cold water. At that time my country was still under the rule of the Japanese. What Korean would have a chance to start a school of any kind for Koreans?

" 'Berea in Korea'!" I repeated. "Dr. Hutchins, you've just given me a million-dollar phrase. But how would I go about it? I wouldn't even know where to begin."

"Why," replied Dr. Hutchins with easy confidence, "just do it with your No. 2 yellow pencil."

I left Berea floating on a cloud. Dr. Hutchins, perhaps without knowing it, had implanted in my heart the seeds of a dream.

It was a dream that would never leave me, that would guide my steps like a beacon, require of me many sacrifices, return to me satisfying rewards—and keep my nose everlastingly to the grindstone.

I was reminded then of a familiar Korean proverb, "If you

want to plan ahead for one year, plant a crop. If you want to plan for ten years, plant a tree. But if you want to plan for one hundred years, build a school."

As the bus bore me away from Berea, my new thoughts hummed with the turning of the wheels.

What could be the meaning of Dr. Hutchins' words—"just do it with your No. 2 yellow pencil"?

I suppose he could mean only that I should write a book. How could *I* write a book? It was about all I could do to give a lecture in the English language. I had learned from my mother, however, that nothing is impossible. If writing a book would help start the school, then I would write a book. I expect that *September Monkey* was born of that remark.

I had many commitments and many problems. There were claims on my time and on my money.

It would be some time yet before I was able to take the first steps toward making my dream of a "Berea in Korea" come true. But from that moment forward, I never forgot it. It never ceased to obsess me. It became my goal; my life now had a purpose.

How great is the power of a dream!

For about a year and a half I continued to travel up and down this country and through every province in Canada speaking for the Student Volunteer Movement. I walked and rode in storms and snows and rain and summer heat.

If my whole life had been laid out in advance with some purpose in mind, this period could hardly have been planned to better advantage, for it was during these months, in towns and cities all over the United States and Canada, that I came to know the many wonderful people who were to become my friends for life. Indeed, it has been these friends who with their love, encouragement, and loyal support have made possible everything that has been accomplished in my name.

It was during this period that I learned the wisdom of the old Korean proverb, "Friendship is like a fence; it must always be kept in good repair."

I have found this to be so true, especially in our time when the pace of life is swift and we all have so many demands on us that a friendship can lapse unless one takes the necessary pains to keep it alive.

For myself, even when I do not have the time to write a long letter, I try to pen a message or a thought of some kind to my friends, even if it is no more than a line or two on a postcard, just to let them know I am thinking of them.

Over the years, I have gained so many friends that now I send more than three thousand Christmas cards to wish them all season's greetings.

Wherever the business of the Foundation takes me now, in this country and in Canada, there is always someone I know, someone ready to take me in, to give me a temporary home, to help me with the planning and organizing of whatever project I have in mind.

Oh, I learned so many things in those years—things that have become of untold value to me. I continued in practice my studies of psychology and sociology in my dealings with people, putting to good use what I had learned in the classroom. I learned many other things, too.

I learned, for example, the importance of being on time. Everything in the United States moves on schedule; the hours are counted, and the minutes, yes, and even the seconds.

I learned to limit my stay to three days because in the United States, the man who comes to dinner stays only for dinner, whereas in Korea the man who comes to dinner in the dry season may still be there eating dessert at the end of the rainy season.

Another lesson which could be learned only through experience was always to travel light. I found it wise never to take more than I could comfortably carry in a suitcase. Sometimes it happened that, in spite of the most carefully laid plans, I would have to walk some distance. A light suitcase presented no problem; a heavy one became an impossible burden.

A bus or a train would be late; a misunderstanding would arise concerning the time of my arrival. If I had heavy suitcases to carry, I would have been in serious trouble.

For traveling light, my native Korean costume was a great asset. The skirt is of plain silk or black velvet. With three or four embroidered silk blouse-jackets, each in a different bright background color of plum, turquoise, or scarlet, I was able to give the impression in my public appearance of having quite an extensive wardrobe.

I enjoyed my work with the S.V.M., and especially the many new friendships which my travels brought me.

But as time went on, more and more people kept coming up to me after my lectures, to tell me that they thought I could get many more engagements if I were on my own. I heard this remark so often that I came to believe it.

Finally I decided to strike out for myself. It took a good deal of courage. But anyone born in the Hour of the Tiger on the Day of the Dragon cannot bear to be confined in any way. I took the plunge.

So began—or rather continued—my life as a gypsy. For many more years, I knew no rest. I had no home of my own. I was the perpetual guest, always smiling, always on my best behavior, always in the public eye, with never a chance to relax or to be myself.

It wasn't that I missed the chance to cry. I'd got past that long ago. Whenever the feeling started coming over me, I would see the strong, tranquil face of my mother at my shoulder and hear her voice saying,

"If it makes you want to cry, don't do it."

In that year also occurred one of the greatest experiences of my life. When I received my itinerary for the spring, I noticed that among the places where I was scheduled to speak, was the First Methodist Church in Wilmington, Illinois.

The name of the town touched a chord in my memory. The first letter I'd ever received from America as a schoolgirl in Korea was postmarked "Wilmington." I remembered now— that was where Mr. C. G. Steinhart lived and his sister, Mrs. W. H. Whitmore. After my mother, they were the two people in all the world to whom I was most indebted. Mr. Steinhart was the blind man who, with his sister, had paid for seven years of my education, three years in Ewha High School and four years in Ewha College.

It isn't always that one has the chance to have such a meeting with one's benefactor. From the moment I read that name on the schedule, I looked forward to this opportunity. Over the years we had written many letters back and forth. But now for the first time we would be talking together, exchanging thoughts in person.

My mind went back in time. Once more I was a thin little girl with big eyes, fresh from a country village in the north, trying to get used to the big city of Seoul. I was getting quite worried as to how much longer I might be permitted to stay in Ewha High School, this nice school I loved so much, when my mother had so little money.

Then I was told the wonderful news. I had been "adopted" by a kind man and his sister in far-off America. It was like this: At that time, people working out of the United States made recommendations to the home missionary society for persons to be helped, especially youngsters to be aided with their education.

Someone at Ewha had heard the story of how I'd gone to school disguised as a boy and had recommended me for a scholarship to Mrs. Whitmore who was chairman of the Woman's Foreign Missionary Society (WFMS) of the First Methodist Church.

When I graduated from high school, Mr. Steinhart and his sister sent me a crisp new dollar bill, the first one I had ever seen. At the time of my graduation from college they gave me my first Bible in English. I kept it with me always, until the time of the Korean War when it was lost, along with everything else I had in the world.

Mrs. Whitmore died a few years ago. At that time her sons sent me her personal Bible. She had always spoken of me as her Korean daughter. I will treasure that Bible throughout my life.

It was a beautiful morning in late April when I got off the bus in Wilmington and went at once to the address given me, that of a modest little white house on a side street.

Mrs. Whitmore greeted me at the doorway with much love and affection. Then she took me into a small, old-fashioned sunny living room. There, in a chair by the window, a cane in his hand, sat a tall, erect man with a strong aquiline nose and a ruddy face and snow-white hair. I don't know exactly what I expected, but one thing impressed me more than anything else: the serene expression on his face. Sightless though he was, he wore a radiant smile.

Without a trace of self-consciousness or self-pity, he reached out a hand in the direction of my footsteps and said, "I'm very glad to see you."

For the next hour and a half we talked, making up for the years in between. It was one of the most inspiring conversations of my life, for, in the course of it, he told me how he had conquered the handicap of his blindness and gone on to live a rich and meaningful life.

He was the son of hard-working, plain-living parents of German descent. At nineteen young Steinhart had an appealing life laid out before him. He was energetic, enthusiastic, and had already given himself to the service of others.

Then in an accident he damaged his eye. Within a short

time he lost the sight of it. Then through the infection of the sympathetic nerve, he lost the sight of the other. Inside of six months he was totally and hopelessly blind.

At first he railed bitterly at his fate, striking out at all those around him.

"I'd much rather die," he used to say, "than be condemned to live out my life in total darkness!"

Only when his rebellion had exhausted him, did he begin to pray. He prayed for three things: that God would give him patience to bear his affliction with fortitude; that he be given spiritual light to replace the vision of his physical eyes; and that he be given the ability to love.

Sitting there in his armchair in the morning sunlight, he said gently,

"And God granted me all those things in full measure."

As soon as peace of mind came to him, he got busy. He learned to type; he mastered Braille; the world opened up to him.

"Today," he told me, "even in my blindness, I am one of the happiest men in the world."

Then he reached for my hand.

"Induk," he went on, "I want you to do this. Every morning when you get up and face the day, don't forget to thank God for your eyes. They are your most precious gift.

"There is only one thing greater—and that is spiritual insight. For what use is it to see if you do not understand?"

He sat up straight in his chair. A look of radiance came over his face.

"This I know: that when I get to Heaven there will be no darkness, and I will see my Master face to face."

He stood up and reached for his sister's arm.

"Do you know where I am going now?" he said with unaffected heartiness. "I am on my merry way to make a talk at the Old People's Home. I am going to tell them your story."

I walked back downtown and got aboard the bus. All the

way to my next lecture engagement in Michigan I thought of that wonderful visit.

I have never forgotten his admonition. Every day since that time when I say my morning prayers I thank God for my eyes.

I received my Master's Degree from Columbia in February, 1931. Already I had an invitation to go to England to speak for the Student Christian Movement.

Therefore, I sailed for England right after graduation. For several weeks I had a wonderful experience, speaking before audiences in schools and colleges.

It was a great thrill for me when I found myself speaking before a women's college at Cambridge University. I noticed many differences between the school systems of England and America. In England there was an air of formality in the relationship between students and faculty, which made me feel more at home, because it was more like Korea.

It excited me, the idea of it—me, a Korean village girl, graduate of little Ewha College, appearing before students at famous Cambridge University.

Later on, when I told my mother, she wasn't particularly impressed.

"What's so unusual about that? I would expect you to do it. You can do anything, you know, if you just set your mind to it."

That was my mother. Compliments from her were hard to come by.

When I spoke at the University of Liverpool, I was delighted to find how much the students knew about my country.

Then came the embarrassing question.

Whereas American students asked, "What about your sports and your music? What's your major industry?" the British wanted to know, "What about your politics?"

At that time we were under the Japanese occupation, and a direct answer would have caused many difficulties for me when I went back home, so I turned the question aside, saying, "Politics absolutely fascinates me. But I am no politician."

When I had completed my speaking engagements in England, I went on to the Continent where I spoke first in Belgium and then in Germany.

But it was in Denmark that I was most stimulated for my future work. This came about through my visit to the International Folk High School. It was there that I discovered the co-ops.

The co-operative system seemed to me the perfect compromise between the free enterprise system of the West and the totalitarian controlled economy of Russia.

Free enterprise is fine if you have the resources. But for poor people without means, something else is needed. The co-op provides the means to make the poor man a capitalist.

I was very impressed by those students at Elsinore, which, by the way, is the real life setting of Shakespeare's *Hamlet*. In seven languages they could tell you, very offhandedly of course, the price of a pork chop. Besides that, they were so happy and looked so healthy.

Something I found pleasing was their constant singing. They sang at the beginning of class and at the end of class, when they came to school and when they left school, before they ate and after they had eaten. And the relationship between the sexes was so sound—separate, but equal; they treated one another with mutual respect.

This was what Korea needed. I could see that. There was no such easy social relationship at home. I must hurry back to see how much of what I had learned in Denmark could be applied to Korea.

3

*

The Needle and the Pencil

THERE I WAS, back home again in Seoul. I hurried as fast as I could to "Inside Grandma's" house. Out in front, playing in the yard, were my two little girls. But they weren't little girls any more! I looked at them in amazement. Iris was now ten and Lotus eight. They had been three and five when I left. I'd been away over five years.

Shyly, they looked up at me, clinging to the skirts of their "Inside Grandma." Finally I coaxed them to come to me. That strong blood bond which exists between mother and daughter asserted itself and gradually we got to know each other again. I felt they were part of me. No one had to tell me how to get acquainted with them—they were mine.

As I played with them, I tried to envision what their lives would be like—what kind of women they would grow up to be. I made up my mind then and there that I would do all I could to help them lead useful lives, to become strong, independent women of their generation, to try to do for them what my mother had done for me.

Now that I was back once more in my own country, I could make a start on the project that had interested me for so long, namely, to help the rural women of Korea.

I had no trouble getting permission from the Japanese officials to travel and teach in the villages, for the war was still some distance away and they were not so particular about what we did.

I spent the summer getting ready. I couldn't start until fall, because the women had their only free time in the winter months after the harvest had been gathered.

I went out into the countryside from my home in Seoul, traveling by train or bus, then walking from village to village.

Coming fresh from my travels through Europe and my long stay in America, the first sight of the primitive condition of life in Korean villages, where nothing had changed in thousands of years, made a profound impression on me.

I had grown up in such a village. I had returned there to visit my mother on vacations, on holidays, and at other intervals in my life.

For that reason I knew the village women well. I knew that in spite of the sparseness and hardship of their lives, their crushing poverty, the shortage of modern conveniences, the lack of personal freedom, they had remarkable attributes of character. They were patient, loyal, and unfailingly cheerful in the face of adversity.

Their spirit is beautifully expressed in a piece of writing of unknown origin which has long been circulated in Korea from hand to hand. It is a eulogy by a certain Mrs. Yu to her needle. I quote it here:

A needle is important to women, but its importance is not recognized because it is so common. This needle of mine, now broken, was different from all the others, for I had it for twenty-seven years. You wonder why I feel so sad to lose it? Some years ago my husband's uncle brought some needles from Peking. I gave some to relatives far and near, and even to some servants. Some I kept.

But I selected this needle and was accustomed to it until this time, while all the other needles broke long ago. Although it was just a needle, I loved it. How much I miss it. It's like a person to me.

My life has been unfortunate, losing my husband and not having a child. I wanted to die—but still live in poverty. This needle came into my possession and comforted me and assisted me with my living. Now we have to be parted forever. This must be the jealousy of a departed spirit.

Dear precious needle, because of its unique beauty, quality, and tact it was noted above all things and outstanding of all steel. It was quick and smart in temperament, strong and straight in character for all these years. Its sharp point and the keen ear looked as if they were ready to talk and ready to listen. When I was embroidering the phoenix on the silk, its quickness and agility were beyond description.

There are times when a child leaves, or a servant disobeys, but it never left me. I kept it in a beautiful silver case and wore it. I used it for stitching, hemming, and quilting near the beaded folding screen in the daytime and under the oil lamp in the evenings. One night at the Hour of the Dog [8:00-10.00 P.M.] on October 10, while I was finishing the Royal Robe [a loose, floating-sleeved robe with a phoenix on the front and a dragon embroidered on the back] under the dim light . . . ouch . . . it broke right in the middle. For a second I was dazed. I put those two pieces together, but it was no use. It was broken. I felt as if an arm or a leg of mine had been amputated. My precious needle! I looked at the place where I used to keep it, but gone! It was no one's fault but mine. Oh, my dear needle, you are gone forever!

I brought with me on my trips a collection of pencils and notebooks. It was my hope, as I went about teaching the alphabet, that I might be able to replace the faithful needle with a No. 2 yellow pencil!

It was my plan to begin by teaching the housewives the

Hangul alphabet so that they could read the Korean language. I would follow up by teaching them basic principles of child care, health, and sanitation. Then I would go on to try to interest them in consumer co-operatives. When I got to know them better I would bring my Bible and read to them, encouraging them to go to church so that they could gain spiritual strength.

When I came back for my second visit I would find that the pencils and notebooks had not been touched. Instead, the housewife would take me to a corner of the kitchen, and there with her poker, she would draw in the hard-baked mud of the kitchen floor the Hangul letters she had learned.

At first I could not understand why she did so. But soon I came to realize that the mother considered pencil and notebook so precious that she wanted to save them for the children in the hopes that they would one day learn to read and write by using them.

The co-operative movement had already been introduced in Korea, largely through Y.M.C.A. and church workers, and was proving quite popular in the villages where it had been tried.

I concentrated on helping the housewives to save money through the principle of co-operative buying. All housewives, I knew, bought some of the same items for their families: soap, oil for the lamps, boots for the children. Why not, I suggested, pool their resources and buy direct from the wholesaler, thus saving the extra money and being able to buy more things?

Every two weeks I returned to see how things were going and to give another lesson. While I did not notice many striking changes in the way they were living, I did notice an enormous improvement in their spirits. The simple fact that they were learning to read and write increased their self-assurance, coloring their whole approach to life. At least that was the only way I could account for the fact that in general they seemed much happier. It gave me pleasure, too, to know that I was doing what I could to help them.

Only, at the back of my mind, one persistent chord of discontent nagged at me: I wasn't doing anything about "Berea in Korea."

My classes grew. Soon I was teaching fifty women from several villages where before I had only fifteen women from one village. But it was hard to find a house that would accommodate so many. Confronted with this problem, I made up my mind to build my own teaching center.

I found a piece of land about thirty miles from Seoul in what is known as the Kimpo area, near where the airport is now. I put up two thatch-roofed cottages: one for teachers' lodgings, the other to serve as a classroom. I called my school the Village Center.

Now the village housewives would have to come to me instead of my going to them. This would save me time and energy and make it possible to reach and teach more women. At the same time, since they had to walk for their education— and quite a distance at that—they would appreciate even more what they were getting.

For a time, everything went along smoothly. Then, with the attack on Pearl Harbor, my activities came to an abrupt halt. The Japanese were opposed to any ideas or any way of expression that came from America. They did not like my going about meeting with village women. They were afraid I might be carrying with me some subversive thoughts.

Just when I had things really under way, I was forced to sell the cottages and the land, and close up my village center.

This was a serious blow to me. I did not like to sit in idleness. My mother, as usual, gave me some good advice:

"Just because you find one door is closed to you, is that any reason to give up? God has in mind another one for you, somewhere. Keep looking around, keep knocking, and you will find it. All you need is the tiniest crack. Through that crack you'll see a light. The light must be coming from somewhere. Follow it—and you'll find out exactly where."

In time, as Mother had said, I found the light for myself. I decided I would start another school—this time one that would not prove disturbing to the Japanese. Mine would be a school in home economics for girls who had finished high school, a productive way to fill the period between graduation and their wedding day.

My plan was to train them in home-making, in the care of husbands. I intended to pay special attention to counseling them on how to get along with their in-laws, for in Korea the woman is still expected to make her home with the husband's family and to devote herself to helping look after his parents. This abrupt confrontation between the old and the new often proved to be the source of much domestic friction, and I wanted to do what I could to lessen or eliminate it. My school was, in fact, designed to prepare girls in every possible way for marriage. In time it proved to be quite popular as a kind of "matrimonial waiting room."

For the next four and one half years while so much of the outside world was racked with agony, Korea, at least so far as the fighting was concerned, remained a quiet backwater. Not that, under the heel of the Japanese, it was exactly a comfortable backwater. All our people, men and women, boys and girls, all but the old and infirm or very young, were drafted into the Army of the Rising Sun or into the labor force, or for work on farms. All of our patriotic leaders, those formerly in key positions, were thrown into prison. Everyone had a struggle just to get enough food to survive.

Our men and boys were forced by the Japanese to work building highways and airstrips, growing more food for them, taking turpentine from the trees for them to burn instead of gasoline. Our workers were driven to the point of exhaustion by their guards who beat them when they faltered. And the outlook for the future seemed darker still.

We knew nothing of how the war was going except what the Japanese told us. And according to them, they were chalking up one victory after another in the Pacific, while their German allies in Europe were beating everybody right and left.

It was during this trying time that my daughter Lotus, like so many other young people, contracted the tuberculosis that was to be the cause of her death.

I was glad that I had my school. At least I was doing something. What kept me going was the firm hope that sometime a better day would come for my country and I was helping my girls to get ready for it.

One hot, sultry morning in August, word came over the radio for everyone to stand by. It was a time of day and that time of year in Seoul when the city was absolutely dead—nothing was being done anywhere.

A few minutes went by. Then we heard a voice, very grave, very solemn. It was the voice of the Emperor of Japan. Incredible as it seemed, he was actually talking to us! Furthermore, he was agreeing to unconditional surrender. That could only mean one thing: freedom for us! But we could not yet believe it.

I had no telephone. We ran out on the street. Everything was still dead quiet. We went to the home of a friend who had a phone. Yes, it was true. Japan had surrendered. We were free! For a few minutes more the quiet continued. Then pandemonium broke loose.

Try to imagine what it was like—the utterly joyous feeling at the end of thirty-five years of Japanese domination. It was as though our entire nation was one big prison and its doors had suddenly swung open. Everyone shouted and sang. People got out the flags they had kept hidden through the years for this very day, and waved them as they ran through the streets. The confusion was indescribable. Refugees, Americans, Russians —all were coming to Korea and the Japanese were going home.

Then on September 9, General John R. Hodge with his Twenty-fourth Corps arrived at Seoul after landing at Inchon. A measure of order was restored. But confusion still continued, however, for three months, until General Hodge set up an American provisional military government to protect Korean independence.

Soon it was announced that the country would hold an election—its first in the four thousand years of its history.

Our women were to have the privilege of voting for the first time. It was a huge undertaking to prepare them to make the best possible use of their franchise.

All at once I had two jobs to do.

As chairman of the political education committee of the Patriotic Women's Society, I was assigned to educate the village women for the vote. I prepared a series of lectures on women's new opportunities and responsibilities under a democracy, delivering a talk over the radio once a week.

At the same time I was asked to give a series of lectures to the GI's on my country, its people, history, and customs. My talks must have been well received for one day General Hodge sent for me and said,

"Since you have had the experience of speaking with the Student Volunteer Movement, I want you to go back to the United States and tell my countrymen about your people, just the way you've been lecturing to the GI's.

"But I do not want you to be a spokesman for the U.S. military government. I want you to be absolutely on your own. We will make it possible for you to go to the United States —that's all."

Three weeks later I left by military air transport on my way to New York City. I slipped naturally back into my life of traveling and lecturing, meeting old friends and making new acquaintances.

From the very moment the war had ended, my dream of founding a "Berea in Korea" became uppermost in my mind. But how to do it? Where to start? First of all, I would have to earn some money. I knew well enough nothing could be accomplished without money.

So I would do the only thing I knew how to do—make speeches. And then—somewhere, somehow—I would write a book: "Use my No. 2 yellow pencil," as Dr Hutchins had suggested.

My first invitation was to attend the United Church Women's Annual Convention in Grand Rapids, Michigan. I was asked as a guest, not as a speaker. My transportation would be paid, but of course there would be no fee.

I was rather disappointed because I was impatient to start saving my first few dollars toward "Berea in Korea." How stupid I was! I should have known by now that God knew how to manage everything. I should have learned to trust in Him.

Mary McLeod Bethune, who was president of Bethune-Cookman College at Daytona Beach, Florida, was to be the key speaker. At the last minute she sent word that she would be unable to come. I was invited to speak in her place.

When I stood up, I was exhilarated. It was my first appearance in the United States as a free Korean. Always before that time I had been forced to exercise extreme caution because we were still under Japanese occupation and my expressions of opinion might be heard at home.

Also, I'd had to limit myself to expressing opinions that were proper for a Korean woman under the old regime.

Now I was completely free; I was as free as a bird let out of a cage. I could say absolutely anything that came to my mind. In fact, I felt so free that at first I hardly knew how to act. I spoke to those women about freedom.

"You never know how precious a thing it is," I said, "until you have lost it."

They must have felt my emotional intensity, for when I sat down they gave me a tremendous ovation.

The consequence of my success was that before I left Grand Rapids on the following day, I had received enough invitations to keep me busy for the next ten months. My big problem now was how to sort them out geographically. I could hardly wait to make the first speech so that I could start putting money in the bank toward "Berea in Korea."

At that time I had no headquarters. The nearest thing to a base was the home of a friend in Oak Tree, New Jersey. To reach it, I had to go into New York then out of it. So I decided the most accessible place for me to open an account would be at the Bowery Savings Bank. I chose a savings rather than a checking account deliberately. I wanted only to put money in—not to take any out.

I had given several lectures and had traveled quite a bit before I made my first deposit. I do not remember exactly how much it was—perhaps fifteen dollars.

But as President Kennedy once said, quoting the ancient Chinese, "The longest journey begins with but a single step."

I had taken mine. The long hard journey toward my goal—establishing "Berea in Korea" had begun.

Then also was the beginning of my life as a gypsy for an uninterrupted period of thirteen years, five months, and five days.

For all that time I never had a pillow I could call my own. The rain never fell on my own roof.

I was at the mercy of my next lecture engagement, and the

bus or railroad timetable. I was the perpetual guest, my chief concern being not to upset the life of my next hostess.

Yes, I learned a lot of things. I learned, for example, always to say, "Don't bother about supper, thank you, I will have had something to eat before I get there." I always said this, even if I hadn't had a bite since morning, because it always worked out better that way.

In my gypsy life I traveled about forty-five thousand miles a year and each year made about two hundred and fifty speeches. When you consider that the lecture season is confined to eight months it is easy to see that I must have given about a speech a day.

All that time I tried to go as quickly as possible from one hostess to another. The weekends were easy. I usually had engagements on Saturdays and Sundays—then again, I don't know quite why, on Tuesdays and Thursdays. But the time from Thursdays to Saturdays was the hardest to fill.

Sometimes I wished I were a tractor. Then, when I didn't work, I wouldn't have to eat. But, alas, I was more like the faithful Korean ox. I had to keep on eating whether I worked or not.

My gypsy life was brightened by the unfailing kindness of those who invited me into their homes and made me feel like one of the family. Whatever they had, they shared with me.

In this way I came to know the true spirit of the people of the North American continent, of the United States and Canada, as few people have the opportunity of knowing them. I came to know their unstinting generosity in giving to anyone who has need of anything, of helping, where help is required, whether it be for a meal, a lodging for the night, or a college education.

I am grateful for those years and for those friends. I am glad I kept that fence in repair at all times to the best of my ability.

Nevertheless, nothing came easily. God seems always to have made it a rule never to give me more than I needed. When I traveled for the S.V.M., I was on salary. When I launched forth on my own, I had no idea how to charge or what to charge. I never brought the subject up and took what was given me.

Sometimes I would be handed a five-dollar bill. But I was so conscientious that before I left a certain city I might have given as many as seven lectures in return for that sum. I would voluntarily go right through the Sunday School and give a talk to every class from the juniors to the adults. If I stayed over on Monday, I would go to the school attended by the children of my hostess and give another lecture there.

I don't know whether I would have had the stamina to keep it up indefinitely if a friend had not sent me a picture of the downtown New York skyline, at a time when the tallest sky-scraper was the Woolworth Building. I was reminded of my No. 2 yellow pencil and how it came from a Woolworth store. Then I thought how that huge skyscraper had been built entirely out of nickels and dimes. I said to myself,

"All right, then, Mr. Woolworth, if you could build a great big skyscraper that way, why can't I at least build a school?"

As I became better known, my honorarium increased—I began to get ten, fifteen, twenty dollars, and later, anywhere from twenty-five to fifty, when I started to name a fee. But it was not as much as it sounded, because the bus fares and meals ate deeply into it.

4

*

"Berea in Korea"

THE YEARS PASSED; I made more and more frequent
trips to the Bowery Savings Bank with my deposits. By living
frugally and tucking away a few dollar bills in my purse, I was
able to put in the bank sometimes five dollars, sometimes
twenty dollars.

"Berea in Korea" still seemed far off in the future. Since
there were so many young people in need who could not be
expected to wait for their education, much of my earnings
went toward scholarships for Korean boys and girls. What
money remained for the long-range project of the school
wasn't as much as I would have liked.

But the time came when I thought I had saved enough to
buy a piece of land in Korea as a site for my school. I knew it
would mean a lot to me to own a piece of land, for it would
bring me that much closer to realizing my dream.

I would like to have gone back to Korea myself to choose
the property. But that was out of the question, as I could not
spare the time just then from my busy lecture schedule. So I

61

did the next best thing; I wrote to my daughter Iris who at that time was making her home in Seoul.

I told Iris that I had by now saved $15,000 which I thought certainly ought to be enough to buy a very good site for the school. So I asked her if she would please go out and scour the countryside to see what she could find.

The site had to be within easy reach of Seoul. That city had been our educational center, the seat of schools and universities down through the centuries. I did not want the boys who entered my school to have the isolated feeling that would come from being stuck off in the country somewhere. Also, I wanted them to be able to enjoy the cultural advantages that Seoul had to offer. I had an idea that land near Seoul might be hard to come by. But I had no idea how hard.

With a new enthusiasm, now that my purchase seemed so near, I continued with my lecture tour while I awaited the good news that Iris had found something for me. I had such a strong feeling that if only I owned a piece of land, "Berea in Korea" would no longer be a fantasy but would be represented by the heading on a bank account. My school, although not yet built, would at least have a home of its own.

All the while I rode the sit-up bus from city to city, the school was never out of my mind. I could see so clearly the location I wanted: The building itself, shining and modern, would be set like a jewel in a grove of pine trees and jutting rocks, possibly on a hillside. Somewhere back on the grounds might be a waterfall; certainly a stream would meander its way through a valley nearby. In the distance would be a vista of friendly mountains.

While I was sitting there painting this vivid picture in my imagination, I would smile happily to myself. Then my seat-mate, if I had one, would look at me in mystification, wondering, no doubt, what flight of fancy could fill me with such joy.

About a month later the letter came in Iris' familiar

handwriting. I could hardly wait to open it. But it was not exactly what I wanted to hear.

"You must remember, Mother," she wrote, "that it has been a long time since you were in touch with things in Korea. You've no idea how land values have gone up—especially in the area around Seoul.

"Your figure of fifteen thousand to purchase the school site in the light of today's prices now appears absolutely impossible. If you are going to find anything which suits you at all, I should say you ought to be prepared to spend about double that amount!"

Double the amount! Thirty thousand dollars!

My heart sank. I thought how hard I had worked, how I had scrimped and saved just to put aside that $15,000.

Do it all over again? Undergo the equivalent of everything I had been through? I found it hard to face up to the prospect.

Well, I had waited this long to get the site for my school. I thought I could wait a little longer. But when I sat down with my No. 2 yellow pencil to work out the figures, I found it was going to take longer than I had anticipated, quite a good deal longer. I did not much like the idea. The tiger is not patient.

Then one day an invitation came to speak once more at Berea College in Kentucky. This invitation came from Dr. Francis S. Hutchins, then president of Berea College.

The invitation stirred memories. So many years had passed since his father had first put the idea of starting a "Berea in Korea" into my head. So much had happened since that time —wars, personal tragedies, small successes.

Thinking about it, I grew depressed. What tangible progress had I made toward my goal in all these years? In view of the bad news I had received from Iris, what chance did I have now ever to realize my hopes. Had I been too optimistic, too ambitious? Had I undertaken something that was beyond my grasp?

I went over again in my mind Dr. Hutchins' dynamic

words, "Why not start a 'Berea in Korea'? Just do it with your No. 2 yellow pencil."

My reminiscence stopped short on that phrase. Yes, that was it! That's what he meant—unmistakably—that I should write a book! I had thought casually from time to time about writing a book and then had pushed the idea to the back of my mind as something I would do someday when I had a little leisure time. Now, when I needed it, the suggestion popped to the surface again.

Visions of best sellers raced through my head. That was the most practical way open to me to add to my lecturing income and thus shorten the time which it would take to earn another $15,000 to buy the land for my school.

Writing was not altogether new to me. I was already the author of three books in the Korean language: a book on the Danish International Folk High Schools, a handbook for rural workers, and a book of essays on my travels in Europe and in America.

It was quite true, I had never attempted to write a book in English. But this possibility did not dismay me. I had been giving lectures in English for so long that I was now able to think in that language without first translating from Korean, in my mind.

I had a story to tell, all right. In many respects my life had been extraordinary. But where to get hold of it? Where to begin?

In preparing topics for my lectures, I always groped for the peak of emotional intensity. Thinking about this stirred my imagination. As I thought back over my own life, what moved me most deeply was the recollection, as a little child, of my mother's grief when my only remaining brother died within one month of my father's death.

I could not help but pause and acknowledge my indebtedness to this brother of mine. I could not know what his life

Mrs. Induk Pahk, the author, has traveled one and a quarter million miles, mostly by Greyhound bus, and has given on an average a lecture a day for eight months out of a year to raise funds for her lifetime dream, the Induk Vocational School for village boys in Korea. Here she is leaving Toledo, Ohio, where she and her project have been "adopted" by the Wesley Service Guild of St. Paul's Methodist Church.

Heron Iris Kim, the author's daughter, was admitted to the United States after three years of trying. Iris is shown here in the backyard of their home in Washington, D.C. with her two sons, Jung Hee and Sun Hee, in August, 1958. Jung Hee was ten at the time, Sun Hee, seven.

Hopeful boys are briefed at the school by the science teacher, Mr. H. K. Park, while waiting to take the entrance examination. Out of 140 boys who applied, there was only room for 30. Mostly poor, many of them refugees, this was probably their only chance at an education.

"Is my name up there?" Names of the lucky boys who had been accepted for Induk Vocational School were posted on a bulletin board just outside. Anxious boys learned of their acceptance—or rejection—by seeing whether or not their names were up there.

Fruit trees play an important part in the farming program, taught as "agri-business." The boys are admiring a peach tree, one of 700 which they hope will be made to bear fruit through artificial pollination. The first year's crop failed because natural pollination did not take place.

In the tractor, which is replacing the faithful ox as the prime source of power, lies to a large degree the farmer's hope for a better tomorrow. "The ox eats whether he works or not," says Mrs. Pahk, "the tractor only when it works." This one-man model is used for plowing and planting as well as for harvesting.

On what the author believes to be the first tour with an ultimate destination in Korea, she takes fourteen American and two Canadian friends on a trip

through the Far East en route to attend dedication ceremonies of Induk Vocational School. The party is about to leave Honolulu for Tokyo by plane.

Rice is the mainstay of the Korean family table. One of the school's important projects is experimentation in new ways of growing rice. Here students are transplanting rice from a dry paddy to a wet one. Two-thirds of the students had never worked in a rice field before.

Landscaping around the school was done by the students themselves under the direction of the science teacher, Mr. Park. Korea abounds in beautiful flowers and shrubs, among them acacias and azaleas. The approach to the school is banked with cosmos, Mrs. Pahk's favorite flower.

The author, Mrs. Pahk, joins students in exalting over the first crop, a yield of new potatoes. Boys work in the fields every afternoon after school, earning part of their tuition. Outdoor work keeps them healthy, and at the same time builds a feeling of self-reliance and independence.

Western sports are popular in Korea. By leveling a hill and grading another part of the grounds, Mrs. Pahk gained space for two athletic fields, one suitable for basketball, soccer, and track, the other for football.

"The crowning day of my life," says Mrs. Pahk, speaking of the ceremonies held to celebrate the opening of her vocational school for boys eight miles out of Seoul. Mrs. Pahk is on a tour of inspection of the school. In the background is the dormitory which houses thirty boys. There is no charge for room and board, but the boys pay two dollars a month tuition.

While Mrs. Pahk continues to travel and lecture to raise money for the school, her daughter Heron Iris Kim has gone to Korea to carry on as the first principal of the school. Mrs. Pahk hopes soon to have accommodations for ninety boys.

would have been, had he lived. But I do know that my life as a woman in Korea might have amounted to very little.

I have always felt that nothing in life comes free. Everything worth while is either paid for by ourselves, or earned for us by the sacrifice of someone else.

Now I had to say,

"Thank you, brother. You have laid on me a great responsibility. Since you have given me the opportunity to write a book, I intend to make it the best I possibly can."

On the afternoon I arrived at Berea, I encountered Leland Stowe. He was about to leave the college, having just completed his lecture, while I was not to deliver mine until the next day.

Mr. Stowe and I had a long visit together. Since he was a successful author as well as a correspondent, I told him all about the book I was planning to write. I asked him for his advice.

The first thing he wanted to know was what I intended to call it.

I told him, more as a joke than anything else, that since I had been born in September in the year designated in the East as the Year of the Monkey, I had thought of calling my book "September Monkey."

His eyes lighted up; I knew I had something.

"Oh, stick to that title, Induk!" he said enthusiastically. "That's a great title! Don't let anyone talk you out of it."

I believed what he said. Besides, I myself had an intuitive feeling that the title was right.

So now I had a title—but no book. It was both exciting and frustrating, not unlike the other position I was in—having part of the money to buy land for a school, but still having no school.

Two years were to pass before I was able to get down to the actual writing. But they were not by any means wasted years.

In the hours I spent riding on buses or waiting to be picked up at bus terminals or railroad stations, the story slowly took shape in my mind.

Then the opportunity came. A dear friend of many years, Mrs. Mary D. Du Bois, had been urging me for some time to spend a summer with her family on their farm called "Hedgefield," located halfway between Salem and Woodstown in New Jersey. It was a lovely place with maple trees, cattle barns, and a rambling old farmhouse filled with spacious rooms. I had often spent weekends there between lecture dates and had thought it might be an ideal place to work on my book.

Late in the spring, while I was still out lecturing, I received another invitation from Mary. This time I accepted.

On the morning I arrived at Hedgefield, I confessed to Mary what I had in mind. Now that the job was staring me in the face, panic seized me.

"Mary!" I blurted out, as guilt-ridden as though I were planning to commit a crime, "I'm going to write a book. And I'm counting on you to help me!"

Immediately, she infused me with a kind of confident calm.

"Of course I'll help you," she said with a quiet smile. "Unpack your things. We're going to start right now. The trouble with books is that people would rather talk about them than write them."

She got a pencil and a notebook. Then we sat together on a sofa in the living room while I told her my story. I told it to her chronologically, starting with my birth in the Hour of the Tiger, the Day of the Dragon, the Month of the Rooster, and the Year of the Monkey. Afterward, we read and studied it together, adding, subtracting, or revising, chapter by chapter.

I soon found how different writing is from speaking. The speaker has many instruments at his command with which to sway an audience—his voice, facial expressions, gestures, movements of the body. The audience can both see and hear at the same time; also, there is the less tangible but more important factor of personal magnetism.

In writing, one had to seek to attain the same results solely through the selection and use of the right word. This task of writing gave me a new respect for the printed word. I could see that the selection of the right one was all-important. What marvelous things words are: When artistically chosen, they are instruments to make people see, hear, experience, feel.

All that summer we worked together, and the book began to take shape. Then I had another bit of good fortune. Through the years, until my daughter Iris came to Washington, the only home I had known was with my friend Velma J. Van Court who lived in Oak Tree, New Jersey. I had a light lecture schedule that winter, so I was able to spend a good deal of time with her.

That year Velma's sister, Mrs. William F. Becker, was living there with her husband. Anna Becker offered her help, and proved to have a flare for the English language. Under the tutelage of Mary and Anna I was able to complete *September Monkey*. With the book almost finished, I had the temerity to begin thinking of a publisher.

Then, in January, 1954, I received a letter from an old friend, Weyman C. Huckabee, general director of the Layman's Movement, inviting me to speak at Wainwright House, in Rye, New York. Mr. Huckabee was the man who had chosen me to be traveling secretary of the Student Volunteer Movement and who had scheduled my lectures. We had kept in close touch through the years.

Among the sponsors of Wainwright House, I noticed the name of Eugene Exman, chief editor of the Religious Books Department of Harper & Brothers, now Harper & Row. I knew then that Harper's was the firm I wanted as my publisher. A meeting was arranged with Mr. Exman, and I submitted my manuscript. After weeks of anxious waiting, a phone call came. *September Monkey* had been accepted conditionally.

Months of revision, working with Margueritte Harmon Bro, my editor, followed. At last the revised manuscript was accepted. On September 10, 1954, I was presented with a copy of *September Monkey* in its finished form.

It had taken me twenty-six years to use my No. 2 yellow pencil as the late William J. Hutchins had suggested. Certainly I did not have another twenty-six years in which to sell my book.

That night I took my copy of *September Monkey* up to my room and dedicated it by inscribing the flyleaf with,

"To 'Berea in Korea'—as yet unborn."

I have written the story of the birth of *September Monkey* chronologically, for the sake of clarity. I see now in looking it over that I may have left the impression that during this period when I was working on *September Monkey,* all was serene and tranquil.

Nothing could be further from the truth. My homeland was torn by the agonies of war, bringing untold suffering to every Korean. None of my fellow countrymen remained untouched by the tragedy.

Four months went by without any word from my daughter Iris. I did not know whether she was alive or dead. I never had a moment of peace.

Then one day, an envelope arrived with an APO number from San Francisco. Inside was a letter from Iris which had been forwarded by a helpful GI. In her letter Iris tried to give me the highlights of what had happened since she had written me last. Her husband had disappeared. He had gone out one morning with five other men to buy some bags of rice and was never seen again.

Not long afterward, the Chinese hordes had swept down across the 38th parallel and Iris, along with most of the populace of Seoul, was forced to flee, despite the fact that she had just given birth to a second son, Sun Hee, three weeks previously.

A cousin of mine was able to get his hands on a jeep in which seven members of the family set out. They included Iris and her two children (Joong Hee was a little more than two years old), my nephew, who later helped me with the school, his sister and his mother, and the cousin.

They made their way to the south along the main highway which was choked with matériel, troops, and refugees. Every time they reached a city they hoped to be able to stop for breath. But everywhere they found the inhabitants had already fled.

They reached Pusan at last, which was at the end of the peninsula. There was no place to go from there but into the sea. It was here that Iris had written her letter. She was quite happy that they had been able to find a place to sleep, even though all seven were occupying one room.

Her letter, though letting me know that she was alive, caused me more worry—she was so far away, with such young babies. I could just imagine that terrible, crowded little room. Would they be able to get enough food? And so it went.

I had no word from her for another two months.

I was still booked heavily, telling Americans about my people and my country. But now that I was in dead earnest about building a "Berea in Korea," I had some practical considerations to think of.

My many friends were both helpful and generous. But we have a saying in Korea: "Even if you have three bushels of pearls, unless you string them you do not have a necklace."

Through my experiences on my travels, I was beginning to find out that I would be seriously handicapped in raising money for the school unless contributions could be made tax exempt. As a matter of fact, I found out that I was earning money for the school the hard way. Everything I was bringing in was classified as personal income on which I was taxed, and at a very high rate. The time had come to make a necklace on which to string my pearls.

The only solution would be to establish a foundation. I read and asked questions and tried to learn how such an organization could be set up. The complications I encountered were discouraging, to say the least. The first and highest hurdle seemed to be that my enterprise could not receive tax-free status until I was able to remain in the United States on a permanent visa. Up to now I had used a temporary visa which I renewed at the proper intervals.

I found out that there were only three possible classifications in which a person could qualify for a permanent visa. One was the claim of immediate family ties—that is, the claim of husband or wife, parents or children. Another was the need for political asylum.

Clearly I had not the slightest chance of qualifying under either of these two categories. Only one remained: A person would be given a permanent visa if it could be shown that his activities were beneficial to the United States. I hardly dared hope that I would ever be able to qualify under that ruling. Still, it was the only possibility, so I set out to work for this.

Then something happened that made the whole business assume a far more critical importance. I received a letter from the immigration authorities advising me that since my temporary visa had already been renewed for the maximum number of times allowed under the law, I would have to show cause why I should be allowed to remain, or I would have to leave the country for good.

That would spell the end for "Berea in Korea." All my education and training had equipped me to earn my living only through lecturing. And even if I had a more marketable skill, money is much harder to come by in Korea than in the States. If I had to leave the country, that would bring my fund-raising efforts to an abrupt end.

Obtaining a permanent visa now became a matter of extreme urgency. In fact, it meant life or death to "Berea in Korea." I began speaking to all my friends about my dilemma. Mrs. Quillian, the wife of the president of Wesleyan College, had a friend whose husband was Georgia Congressman James C. Davis. Word was passed to him, and he agreed to see what he could do to help.

For over a year he worked like a Trojan on my behalf. Meanwhile, my other friends from all over the country did their part by bombarding their own Congressmen with letters and telegrams concerning my plight. I kept holding off the officers of the immigration department by telling them that my application for a permanent visa was pending, and I kept assuring them that I would have some word for them very soon.

Finally, by the passage of a private bill on my behalf sponsored by Congressman Davis, I was granted a permanent visa in July, 1955. I looked on this as an honorary degree from the U.S. Congress. I wanted to do my utmost to justify America's expression of faith in me.

Now I could proceed. With the help of my lawyer, David Carliner, I set up the Berea in Korea Foundation, a nonprofit organization which was born in September, 1955. The officers whom I appointed were all located along the eastern seaboard so as to be available for meetings. No one whom I approached refused. All accepted eagerly.

As we were leaving the first board meeting, one of the members handed me a check. I put it in my handbag with thanks, but without looking at it. When I later took it out, I saw that the amount was $1,000. We were certainly off to an auspicious beginning.

5

*

Instant Family

THE MONTHS FLEW BY; the savings account grew—
but never fast enough. I added more friends to my growing list
of school supporters. Everything went well the next year and a
half. My lecture months were solidly booked, and *September
Monkey* was much in demand.

Then, one day in February, 1957, I was in Fort Lauder-
dale, Florida, on a speaking tour when my friend and hostess,
Mrs. Easter L. Gates, summoned me to the telephone.

"Seoul is calling you, Induk."

For a moment I felt a twinge of alarm. I could only think
that some disaster must have occurred for anyone to be calling
me over a distance of 8,000 miles.

Then I heard the voice of my daughter Iris, as clear and full
of joy as the morning song of a bird.

"Is that you, Mother? Prepare yourself. The boys and I are
coming to make our home with you. We will arrive in Washington on March 4 at eleven thirty at night. I hope you will be
at National Airport to meet us. Good-by."

She had hung up. I'd had no chance to say anything besides

"Hello," for Iris had a great respect for the expense of international phone calls.

I couldn't believe it; they were actually coming. This was one of the happiest moments of my life. Not only would my daughter be coming to live with me, but my two grandsons whom I had never even seen. My days of lonely wandering, during which I had no place to call my own, would be over.

I was, however, totally unprepared to have such a wonderful thing happen to me. For three and a half years Iris had been trying to enter the United States. She had refused to come without her two boys, and for one person to be granted three passports was almost unheard of at that time. The possibility had seemed so slight that I had put it almost out of my mind. And now my family would actually be here. I couldn't seem to get my bearings.

Then suddenly I thought to myself that I should not be saying, "Dear me! What shall I do? I'm about to have a family." I should be saying, "How happy I am—how happy for Iris!"

I had been so concerned about my own dream, that I was forgetting for the moment that when Iris reached America her dream of a lifetime would be well on its way to coming true. Iris' dream was to fulfill herself in music. And her idea of fulfillment was twofold. She wanted to own a piano, and she wanted to be able to play the pipe organ.

For twenty-five years, all the time she was growing up, Iris had longed to have a piano of her own. I could never afford to buy one for her; she could never afford to buy one for herself. She did all her practicing at Ewha School, or sometimes at the home of a friend.

Since childhood, she had loved the pipe organ. Being deeply spiritual, she regarded playing the organ as a form of worship. But since there are very few pipe organs in Seoul, she rarely had a chance to play on one.

Now that she was coming to the United States, next to educating her sons, the most wonderful opportunity for her would be to continue her music studies. Surely now I would be able to buy her a piano on the installment plan. And at least we dared hope that someday, somewhere, a mighty pipe organ would respond to her touch.

But I was still weighed down by a looming sense of responsibility. I had grown accustomed to my gypsy life. For years I'd no one's interest to consider but my own. Now, all at once, I was being called on to create a home. Where should it be?

I had no difficulty in deciding on Washington, D.C. I have always felt that the United States revolves around two cities—commercially around New York, politically around Washington. And Washington is a city of winners. The losers have to move elsewhere.

Also, I liked the idea of being where I could visit the Lincoln Memorial whenever I wanted to. I have seen many famous places, but the most impressive and inspiring scene I have ever gazed upon is the Lincoln Memorial, as seen from the Mall, all lit up at night.

Then, too, I am fond of the changing seasons which remind me of Seoul: the cherry blossoms, the forsythia and azaleas in spring, the lovely snowfalls of winter, and the myriad colored leaves of autumn.

I went at once to Washington and started my house hunt, for I did not have much time. It did not take me long, for God was with me.

In the northwest part of the city I found a modest brick and stucco dwelling, with a rather large living room and fireplace, and a small dining room adjoining the kitchen. It had a pine-paneled rumpus room for Iris' two boys, with a screen porch in the rear looking out over a big backyard where they could play. There was also a den which I could use as an office.

I only had time to assemble the most rudimentary furniture.

Then the day came when it was time to meet Iris and the boys at the airport.

The big plane roared in and pulled slowly to a stop. Eagerly I scanned the faces coming down the ramp. There was Iris, animated and smiling. And there were my two grandchildren, Joong Hee, nine, and Sun Hee, seven. I was filled with thankfulness as I saw how vigorous and full of high spirits they were. Had it not been for the grace of God and the courage and resourcefulness of their mother, they, too, might have been among the millions of poor Korean orphans. How wonderful, I thought, that God had brought us all together once more under His care, safe and sound, to continue our family's destiny.

The two boys threw themselves upon me at once. Proudly using their new-found language, they each demanded a dime which I promptly gave them. (They had learned the word in Hawaii, but had been unable to wheedle one out of their mother the rest of the way to Washington!) The boys had been told all about their "Outside Grandma" whom they had never seen. In Korea, the father's mother is spoken of as the "inside grandma," the mother's mother as the "outside grandma," another indication of the stress placed upon the importance of the male in our society.

I brought my little family to the home I had acquired for them. For the boys the greatest excitement lay in the light switch with which they could turn off both the upstairs and downstairs lights. We all went to bed very shortly, exhausted by the emotional impact of our reunion.

In the morning we had breakfast together. The boys disliked the milk, being totally unaccustomed to it. For lunch they had peanut butter sandwiches which they devoured, despite the fact this was the first time they had ever tasted them. For our dinner, Iris prepared a Korean style meal.

A number of people have asked how we Orientals cook rice. It is really very simple. We wash the rice with cold or lukewarm water a couple of times. Then, putting the rice in a heavy pot, we add twice as much water as there is rice. If we are cooking a large quantity of rice, we use a little less water. We turn the flame high until it boils vigorously, then turn the flame as low as possible, with the lid on the pot, and let it steam for about half an hour. We do not use any salt on the rice because our side dishes are hot and salty. With our rice we serve a dish called *kimchi*. We make that with cabbage or turnips, mixed with salt and pepper, some onions, peppers, a little bit of garlic, pears, chestnuts, and ginger. For us, rice and *kimchi* take the place of bread and butter. One will always find them on the table, three meals a day, in a Korean household. For our first Korean dinner together we had no *kimchi*. It has to be marinated for two or three days to bring out the flavor.

In the evening we had our family prayer. I was pleased to see how well Joong Hee could read the Korean Bible. Each one of us said a brief prayer and then we closed by repeating the Lord's Prayer together. Soon the boys went to bed, and Iris and I sat and talked for a while.

But I scarcely had time to get acquainted with my family. After just one day with them, I had to resume my lecture tour. I had some misgivings about leaving them alone, since Iris and the boys spoke hardly a word of English. I did, however, have some Korean friends in Washington who could look after them, and anyway, I had no choice.

I was gone for two weeks. All the while I was anxious to know how my little family was making out in my absence. But at last I was home. Iris and the boys were so glad to have me back. They had lived more or less in isolation, owing to the language barrier. Our next-door neighbor, however, had two sons about the same age as our boys, and somehow they managed to get along very well by using sign language. All of our neighbors have been very kind to us.

The day after I got home Sun Hee asked me something very touching. He said, "Outside Grandma, what am I going to do if you get old and die and Mama gets old and dies?"

Evidently he felt some insecurity in this new and strange environment.

"You needn't worry, Sun Hee," I assured him, "for you will grow up and become a man before your Mama and I die."

After about three weeks, I took the boys to Lafayette Elementary School, a block up the street. We were lucky to have such a fine school so close by. Joong Hee was assigned to the third grade, and Sun Hee to the first. The principal, Margaret K. Patterson, greeted me warmly; she told me she was pleased to have my grandsons in her school. I explained that they did not know English. She smiled and said she had had many children from foreign lands who had faced the same situation, and she assured me the boys would soon learn.

Miss Patterson taught the Burrall Class at Calvary Baptist Church in Washington. At my first opportunity I attended her class one Sunday, and it looked almost like a church service, for there were over one hundred and sixty women present. Since then I have tried to go once or twice a year, around Easter and Christmas, to hear her and to meet her members. She was anxious that they do something toward the furtherance of my work.

About that time a young student from Korea, with only $100, was dropped in my lap, so to speak, without any warning. He is the son of a friend. During the political upheaval, his father lost everything he had. So I told Miss Patterson of this young man's predicament, and she in turn presented the case to the Class Committee. It was voted on and the unanimous decision was to help him. His welfare would be the Burrall Class project for that year. The class contributed $500 toward his education and gave him many presents at Christmas.

Besides all this, one year on the first Sunday in May her class presented me with a check for $1,000 to be used for "Berea in Korea." It made me very grateful.

Once again, just before I was to leave home for a speaking tour, Iris prepared a typical Korean dinner for us. She had made *kimchi,* of course, and cooked rice, and she broiled the beef according to our style of cooking. She bought chuck roast and sliced it thin. Then she marinated the beef for a couple of hours in a blend of soy sauce, pepper, Wesson oil, sugar, chopped onion, and a little garlic. Afterward, the meat was grilled directly over the fire. We call it *bulgoki,* meaning 'fire meat." It's best to eat it as you are broiling it—it should be sizzling. Nothing can surpass it!

The most important problem which Iris now faced was the necessity to learn English. Soon after we had settled down in Chevy Chase, three women came to see us. One of them, Jane Crawford, happened to be a schoolteacher. She took an interest in Iris and offered to teach her English in her spare time. Miss Crawford taught her how to carry on easy conversations when meeting people and the names of foodstuffs so that she could do her marketing, etc.

It gave Iris a great lift to know there was someone she could call upon for help when the occasion arose. Jane Crawford was a real friend. Her mother, too, was a mother to all of us. my family was more or less adopted by her; she loved us and we loved her. In general, I have found that American people have a predilection for helping those in need, especially the ones who are gifted and talented in some way, but too poor to pursue their education unaided.

In September, Iris registered at the Americanization School, not too far from our home. Apart from taking care of her household duties and looking after her two sons, Iris put

all of her time and energy into her studies. I could see the
progress she was making each time I returned home from a
trip. In six months the boys, too, did amazingly well with their
English.

6

∗

A Caller at the Door

THAT WAS A beautiful autumn morning in Washington, D.C. The date was November 17, 1958. I have reason to remember it well.

I had been spending a few happy days between lecture engagements at home with Iris and the boys. But my brief holiday was almost over. I had just finished packing my things and was getting ready to leave once more when the doorbell rang. A man was standing there whom I had never seen before.

"Are you Induk Pahk?"

"Yes I am."

He drew a folded paper from his pocket and handed it to me. I noticed that it was bound in blue paper and had a formidable legal look to it.

"What is this?" I asked in puzzlement.

"You'd better read it," he said without answering my question.

My eye skipped rapidly down the page. There was no misunderstanding its import. I was being summoned to appear in court to answer charges being brought against me.

"What does that mean—usury?"

"Usury," he explained, "means charging interest in excess of the legal rate."

I told him that I still did not understand what it was all about. He seemed to feel some pity for me.

"If I were you," he said, "I'd consult a lawyer without delay."

He tipped his hat and hurried down the steps as though anxious to be gone.

I was still so stunned I could not entirely grasp what had happened. But certain consequences of what I had read did telegraph themselves to my confused brain as I said to myself:

"I'm penniless . . . everything gone . . . my school . . . now it will never be . . . the work of all those years . . . I didn't do what he said . . . he was my friend . . . I trusted him . . . why is he saying all these things against me?"

Blow after blow after blow. But what hurt me most of all was the realization that I had been betrayed by one whom I had counted among my closest and most trusted friends.

This is the chain of events leading up to the catastrophic situation in which I found myself:

For the first four or five years of my lecturing, I had been putting every cent I could scrape together into a savings bank. Then one day, an old friend whom I had known in Korea called me up. He wanted to know whether I had any money to invest. I said I did have some money, about three thousand dollars. Then he told me he had recently gone into the investment business. He said he knew of several opportunities where my money could earn much more—at least twice as much as it was earning in the savings bank.

This sounded like good news to me. The money for my school had come hard and slowly. If there was any way to turn the dream school into a real school a little faster, I was all in favor of it.

I had no reason not to trust my friend. I had no reason to

be suspicious of him. Since I was a woman, and one from another land and another culture, I had often gone to him for advice on financial affairs, and his advice had always been sound. I had never known him to do anything dishonest. So I did not hesitate to turn all my funds over to him to invest.

For a while he sent me my interest periodically in cash. One day he asked me to go out with him to have a look at an office building. He said that he could make my money earn more if I went in with him and some others to buy this office building. It appeared to be in good condition and well occupied, so I did not see why I shouldn't.

The years went by. I worked harder than ever and turned over to him what I could save to add to my investment. After a while, I stopped receiving any interest in cash. I let it go. But finally I called up my friend and asked what had happened.

"I'm sorry," he said apologetically, "I've been meaning to call you. I had the chance to put us both into the construction business. From now on, you'll be earning fifteen per cent with that portion of your capital."

"But how is it that you are able to charge such a high rate of interest?" I wanted to know.

"That rate is customary for such unsecured loans," he assured me. "The people we are dealing with are most reliable. You have no cause to worry. Just leave everything to me."

The whole affair made me rather uneasy. But my lecture business was crowding in on me; I was traveling most of the time, and did not have the opportunity to pay the matter close attention.

That was how things stood on the morning the process server came to my door.

The language in the summons, although hard for me to believe, was unmistakable. My friend was suing me for 15 per cent interest on all my money which he claimed to have invested in the construction business over a period of years. Why, that would amount to as much as I had entrusted to him from the beginning.

Then another revelation came to me. He had been deceiving me. He had taken my money with the intention of using it to make money for himself.

It was the worst blow I had suffered in my life since the death of my younger daughter Lotus.

I sat down at the dining-room table. After a while Iris came in. She seemed astonished to see me sitting so still. Then her eye fell on the blue-covered summons and she read it quickly.

"Why, don't you see what he's up to, Mother?" she asked. "He's striking first. In other words, he's suing you before you can sue him."

Now I could see clearly the reason for the summons: The best defense is an offense.

I did not sleep that night—nor for many a night afterward. From time to time I was informed that the case in court was going in my favor. But I took little interest in it.

I went on with my lecture tour because the dates had all been made and I had to keep them. But I was hardly aware of what I was saying. Often I did so badly that I felt I owed my hostess an apology. I no longer had any incentive for I knew now that my school could never be. It was too late to start over.

Meanwhile, I was consumed with my hurt. It obsessed me day and night. I tried to remember that I was a good Christian and to refrain from harboring hate in my heart. But I could not help from dwelling on my hurt.

Over and over again I asked myself, "God—why?"

All my life I prided myself on my self-reliance. I had thought I would be able to surmount any disaster—to face any catastrophe with calm. I thought this because of my inherited strength of will, grounded in my firm faith as a Christian.

I had always said to myself, "I am a Christian. I have faith."

I had never had occasion to ask myself, "But how *strong* is my faith? How *complete* is my reliance on God?"

Now in those months of my suffering, I made a deeply disturbing discovery about myself. My faith was not strong enough to sustain me in the face of serious adversity.

So what to do? I prayed. I prayed again and again. And I waited. But no solace came.

Vaguely I was aware that when one is in such a state of mind, it cannot possibly continue forever. One knows that something simply must happen. A point is reached where one turns upward—or dies.

I knew that for me such a point could not be far off when I received a letter from a friend. A group of women were going on retreat at an Episcopal Conference Center in western Massachusetts beginning the 7th of May and wanted me to join them.

I had an intuitive feeling that this invitation was some kind of message. I accepted eagerly.

I arrived with the others at a spacious wooded estate. On the grounds was a weathered, many-gabled old house where we would be staying. On the ground floor of the house was a small, intimate chapel, where tapers burned beside an altar day and night.

This was the first I had ever known of the magic of spring in New England. Everything was rich and fresh and fragrant and green. On all sides were the deep yellow of the forsythia, the red and pinks of the azaleas, the light blue of the hydrangeas, all bright against so many, many shades of green—from the somber blue-green of the pine trees to the light, lacy, yellowish green of the willows.

Everywhere I looked I saw rebirth—the surge of new life. But there was none within me, only a heavy emptiness.

The retreat began with a pleasant social time for the eighteen ladies who were there. Soon the moment came to enter upon our retreat in earnest. To intensify our concentration we put into effect our vow of silence.

If any one of us wanted tea or coffee, or salt at the dinner table, she simply wrote out the request on a slip of paper and passed it down.

Every evening after supper I went down on my knees before the altar, praying in the candlelight. From time to time in the cavernous depths of the house, came the most musical sound. A grandfather clock was chiming the hour. It had an almost spiritual sound, rich and echoing as it went winging through the silent house. But the chime, too, failed to stir an answering echo in me.

And then—on the evening of May 14, it happened, just as I have described it in my opening chapter. When the clock struck midnight, it stirred old memories and aroused an echo in me. I was ready. My rebirth had come.

I could look back now and see what had been happening. I had been unburdening my soul of all its hurts and hates. I was preparing myself. When the ugly voice startled me, I was no longer defenseless.

From the strength of my assertion "It can be done! It *will* be done!" I knew that I had reached bottom and had started upward.

I remained motionless while the beating of my heart grew steadier. But I had hardly spoken the words when a strange light appeared in the room, filling it with an unearthly radiance. I remember that it was a kind of velvet blue, the color of a night sky, with overtones of deep purple.

Then I noticed that the light, while hovering, had a definite shape. It was rectangular. I saw that it was filled with curious geometric figures and designs which were unfamiliar to me.

For a moment the light hung in midair, pulsating vibrantly. It lingered a little—then it was gone. All was quiet, all was calm in my soul. I slept in deep peace through the remainder of the night.

I awoke in the morning to the full glory of a New England spring: the rippling of sunlight, the fragrance of budding blossoms, the lilting songs of the birds. Now it was my spring too, for I had become a part of it.

Above the general chorus of bird trills I heard one note of ineffable sweetness. I recalled a friend who is a nature lover having told me that the bluejay, whose cry is usually raucous and harsh, also has a beautiful liquid note that he reserves for his love song. I felt certain that must be the note that I was hearing now.

I went to the window and looked out. Then, as naturally, as spontaneously as the birds themselves, I, too began to sing:

> I sing because I'm happy
> I sing because I'm free
> For His eye is on the sparrow
> And I know He watches me.

I could sing again! Once more I had peace of mind. What is to be treasured above peace of mind! If we do not have it, nothing else matters very much. If we do have it, we can get along with little in the way of material things. Now once more I had it. With it, I knew that everything else would all come right again in its own good time.

I did not consciously change any plans for the future. I did not say to myself, "I will try once more to make 'Berea in Korea' a reality and this time I know how to do it."

I did no more than continue with my life. But this time I did so with confidence.

A few days later I was scheduled to speak before an audience of women at a Congregational church near Boston. I don't know why I did it or what happened but the moment

I stood up there I said something quite different from what I planned to say. I began quite simply,

"I want to tell you a little of what it has meant to me to know Jesus Christ as my Friend and Savior."

I went on, speaking from the heart. I could feel that electric current flow between the audience and me. All the suffering I had experienced and my struggle to recover had given me new depth, and this I was now able to communicate.

As the insight matured within me, for the first time I could see where I had made my mistake, where I had gone wrong. My faith, my spirituality, had not been strong enough to carry me through. I did not know this until I was tested. I had not relied sufficiently on God. Now I was strengthened. I was armored.

When I had finished speaking, the ladies crowded around, congratulating me with an enthusiasm greater than any I had ever known before. I felt within me the wellsprings of a new power.

At first I thought this might be an isolated experience, coming as close as it did on the heels of my spiritual renewal. But it happened again. And again. It was not just chance. I had indeed become a new person, and a more forceful speaker.

A few months later when I had an engagement at a church in Florida, it was suggested that instead of speaking for a fixed fee, I ask for a voluntary donation. Now I had the confidence to do it. When the collection was counted I found, to my amazement, that it amounted to $580!

At last I could dare to dream of "Berea in Korea" again. If I could prevail in a manner like that, it was not too late after all. I did have time within my life to see it realized. The Korean village boys would not be robbed of their chance—not if I could help it. I could help it—and I would!

The tiger within me who had been asleep stirred and stretched. Now that I dared think of my school again, I worked like a woman possessed. I went from one speaking date to another as fast as I could. I abandoned altogether my practice of speaking for a fixed fee and relied completely on the generosity of my audiences.

The results were like magic. Where once I had worked and struggled to make five, ten, fifteen dollars, now each appearance brought in several hundred dollars.

And then something new and wonderful began to happen. Friends, whose interests had been aroused, started sending me checks to be added to the school fund. It seemed almost miraculous, but my savings account was growing once more and growing by leaps and bounds.

7

*

"What Are Those
Tall White Things?"

EXACTLY TWO YEARS to the day after my spiritual re-
awakening, I was to leave once more for Korea. This was the
15th of May.

My train left Washington at three in the afternoon. I
planned to stop off in New Jersey to have a last visit with my
friends there. When I got off at Iselin, Velma Van Court was
there to meet me. She had a solemn look on her face.

"Pahky!" she greeted me. "I've just heard on the radio that
a revolution has broken out in Korea."

I gave an exclamation of surprise, for I'd had no inkling of
any special trouble brewing. Velma told me that the fighting
began at the very hour I left Washington.

"Surely you're not going now, are you?" she demanded.

"Oh, yes, I am. I'm on my way."

"Pahky, don't be so stubborn! You can't do business during
an uprising. You know that."

"I'm not turning back," I said. "Nothing can change my mind."

While we were having dinner, Iris called me from Washington.

"I suppose you've heard the news."

"Yes, I've heard it."

"You've canceled your plans, haven't you?"

"Nothing of the sort. I'm going right ahead."

She then quoted one of the old Korean proverbs, "Only a fool would jump into the sea with a bag of salt on his back, or leap into a fire with a load of gunpowder."

Usually I pay attention to my daughter's advice. She is more realistic, more practical-minded than I am and less inclined to be impulsive and headstrong. But this time I had to make up my own mind.

"Dear child," I said, "I am in God's hands. Now take good care of yourself and the boys."

I hung up before she could argue with me any further.

I took a Greyhound bus to the west coast, spending two nights and three days on the road. The two old friends who were to fly across the Pacific with me, Mrs. Easter L. Gates and Mrs. T. L. Marquis, met me in San Francisco. They were no more concerned than I was by news of the revolution. We had made plans for our trip long ago and did not intend to cancel them now.

We paused for a few days to enjoy Honolulu, then went on to Japan, landing at Haneda Airport in Tokyo seven hours after take-off.

The first thing I did was to try to find out what was happening in my country. But censorship had clamped down tight. I could learn nothing and so had to resign myself to waiting.

We'd had the good fortune to arrive in Japan at harvest time. This was a wonderful opportunity to see something of the countryside so we hired a car and set out. The farmers were gathering in the wheat and also planting their rice fields.

The fields, with their neat checkerboard pattern of greens and browns, made an attractive picture, with not an inch of space wasted.

Everywhere we went we saw tractors in use, for plowing as well as for harvesting. I was intrigued to see the farmers using tractors to transport themselves back and forth between villages and fields.

Our guide remarked that never before in the country's history had farmers been so prosperous, and I could believe it. The size of the average farm in Japan today is around two and a half acres. Ever since the land reform following World War II, the farmer has been permitted to own as much land as he can pay for and utilize productively, which partially accounts for the improvement in his status.

I was especially interested when I was told that in Japan today the daughters of farmers confidently expect to own refrigerators, washing machines, and TV sets. If it were possible for farmers in Japan to become so prosperous, then why couldn't Korean farmers do likewise? It could happen, I was convinced, once my countrymen learned how to practice farming as a business. This was one of the aims of my school. I could hardly wait to get back there and get on with it.

The most memorable experience of this particular visit was our journey to Nikko, the picturesque home of ancient shrines located in the mountains about one hundred miles to the north of Tokyo. A friend of ours, the Rev. Jeyoul Whang, a Y.M.C.A. secretary from Korea, had offered to drive us there.

The trip up the mountainside with its thirty hairpin turns was spectacular. Getting to see the magnificent Buddhist Temple was the climax of this excursion. I had heard that some Korean architects had contributed to its construction and I thought I could see traces of their handiwork.

At Nikko, too, can be seen the originals of the three

monkey figures which have become famous the world over as "See no evil; hear no evil; speak no evil."

"If there had been a fourth monkey," said Easter, "it would have been called 'Mind your own business'!"

Everywhere we went I saw evidence of the new role the Japanese are assuming in the world today. They are the courteous hosts to visitors from all over the world coming to enjoy the beauties of their country and their customs. Today they seem to take as much pride in their mastery of the art of hospitality as they once did in their bravery as warriors. They seem to be able to handle any number of visitors with aplomb. Children as well as adults go out of their way to make visitors comfortable.

From Tokyo we flew to Hong Kong. We found this city fascinating not only because of its natural beauty, but because of the contrasts caused by its position as a confrontation point between the Free World and the Communist World, between West and East.

We felt the pressures of so many people trying to make a living in that small space. As soon as we were through customs crowds of Chinese surged forward, trying to be of service. They were hopeful but polite. They offered to get us rickshas or taxis, restaurants or hotels.

Fortunately, we already had our reservations at a new hotel, the Hamilton, which had been recently opened in Kowloon, a strategic location for tourists.

That evening, as soon as we had settled into our new quarters we went to the Aberdeen Fishing Village in Hong Kong Harbor for a fish dinner. We were shown live fish of all shapes, sorts, and sizes caught from the bay and kept in tanks. We were invited to choose the ones we wanted to have served to us. Soon they were brought to our table, steaming on a bed of seaweed.

As we ate, we watched the hum and bustle of life going on

aboard the junks in the harbor all around us, and listened to the strange sounds and cries. Literally thousands of Chinese make their homes on junks such as these. The colonies of sampans are as characteristic of the Chinese as trailer parks are of Americans.

The best of them, we were told, cost anywhere from four to five thousand dollars up. Here, in their floating homes, Chinese are born, grow up, get married, live and die. Some of the craft we saw evidently were home to three generations at the same time.

Across the water, a large family was seated around a low table on deck, having the evening meal. Each member was holding a bowl of rice and the chopsticks flew. All were talking and laughing at once, obviously enjoying themselves.

The sight of them set me to thinking—what is happiness? From what I could see, this family had little in the way of worldly goods; yet they appeared to be more content than others I have known with more status, more material wealth. Warmth, mutual affection, strength of family ties—all these intangibles go further toward creating happiness than material goods, I am sure.

On the following day we drove to the New Territory. This is the point where Free China comes closest to the mainland of Red China; only a narrow river separates them.

As we looked, we saw a little Chinese junk go floating slowly by, as though altogether unmindful of the political strife. Centuries pass, I thought, and life on the river does not change. Yet it is from across the river that hordes of refugees have descended upon Kowloon.

I was appalled to see them in such numbers—thousands upon thousands of them crowded together in the resettlement areas. Their condition is pitiful, since they lack not only the most primitive comforts, but also food and sometimes even water.

Where are provisions to come from? Who, I thought, will

supply the five loaves and two fishes? Our heartfelt thanks went out to the Christians of America and Canada, who, along with the British government, have been doing what they can to relieve this sad situation.

It surprised me to learn that Red China owns a big bank in Hong Kong and that trains run between Hong Kong and Red China. I was also told that a vast smuggling trade is plied between the two countries. When a friend of mine invited us all to lunch at a Cantonese restaurant, I asked her why Red China didn't help herself to Hong Kong, in view of the situation.

"To begin with," said my friend, "Hong Kong would not be easy to take. But more than that, Hong Kong is Red China's nose and throat through which she breathes out into the free world and breathes in from the free world. Without Hong Kong, Red China would suffocate. No, I do not think she would want to take Hong Kong."

Our next stop was Singapore where we stayed at the Raffles. This hotel, famous in both history and literature, was named for the renowned British statesman and adventurer. It is a picturesque, rambling old structure, with a spaciousness rare in more modern hotels. Our room was Number 23. It had once been occupied by Marilyn Monroe, so the desk clerk told us. We each took possession of a corner and made ourselves at home. But the distance between our beds was so great and the buzzing whir of the electric fans so loud that we had to shout to make ourselves heard from our beds.

In the morning we went outside to see a cobra dance. It was very hot; nevertheless, two Indians squatted on the ground and played music so that the snake would dance and sway. But the poor reptile only raised its head wearily, then flopped back into the basket. The fakir got busy and tried to make the cobra perform by sprinkling cold water on it. However, it was of no use.

We flew directly from Singapore to Manila. I was pleased to learn that my country now maintained an embassy there. I was told that the husband of a friend of mine had been the ambassador, but had only recently been replaced because of the revolution.

After some sight-seeing in Taiwan and Okinawa we started home for Seoul by way of Tokyo. At that time the flight from Tokyo took three and a half hours; by now it has been reduced to less than two hours. I still didn't know what conditions we might encounter upon landing.

It was not long after we zoomed in from the sea that I spotted Nam Sam (South Mountain), which is shaped like the head of a silk worm. Characteristically green at this time of year, it wore its blanket of lovely trees. At its foot was the thin blue ribbon which I knew to be the Han River.

Now, below me, I could make out the pattern of the city of Seoul. A great warm feeling came over me. This was the land where I was born. I was home again. At exactly 3:30 P.M. on June 29, 1961, the plane touched down. I was curious as to what I would find for I had no information as to what the situation would be, but everything was peaceful and orderly. There was hardly a soldier in sight and no sign of revolutionary activity. Thank goodness the uprising was over and done with. A crowd of friends and relatives had gathered at the airport to greet me. They called out, "Welcome home, Grandma!" or, "Oh, Auntie, it's so good to have you back." It was the warmest welcome I could have possibly hoped to receive. There must have been more than a hundred people in that crowd at Kimpo Airport.

I was delighted by the kindness and courtesy with which my countrymen received my traveling companions from the States.

When we got through customs that day, we were greeted by a downpour, which meant the rainy season had begun. I am always running into rain, but I should not be surprised. What else could be expected when one is born under the sign of the Dragon?

I began to feel at home during the thirty-mile trip from the airport in the ramshackle taxi made from a reconditioned jeep. All around us were homemade buses, their bodies encircled with stripes of vivid color, their engines coughing and chattering noisily. The streets along which we passed, the houses, the stores and restaurants, the people on the sidewalks, were all touchingly familiar to me. They had been a part of my life for so long.

The following day I went to visit the First Methodist Church which had always meant so much to me. It had been wrecked by bombing during the war but was now renovated and restored. Next door to the church stood the Jensen Memorial Building. It had been erected in honor of Chris Jensen of the Methodist Mission who had been captured by the Communists when the Red Army marched into Seoul in June, 1950, and who later died.

Just beyond the church was Ewha High School. It was the first time I'd been there since the Korean War. What powerful feelings overcame me as I recalled the happy days I had spent there, the friends I had made. After all, it had been my home for eight years. I wandered around the campus, trying to orient myself.

That red brick building where I had spent so much of my girlhood had vanished altogether. I remembered someone having told me that it had been totally destroyed. Yes, it must have stood right here where there was now only an expanse of smooth green lawn. I looked for familiar landmarks. Only the stone steps, which I had once run up so merrily, remained, sagging a little now.

So much was gone of former times—not only the places, but the people. My own dear daughter Lotus . . . the husband of my daughter Iris . . . so many good friends.

My glance went out, beyond the campus. There was a wide modern boulevard, rebuilt since the war. Many fine new modern buildings were going up on both sides of the street. I heard the sound of happy voices and noticed children playing there, some intent on their games with pebbles, others laughing, chattering, or quarreling.

And I realized then that there was much to be proud of, much to be thankful for. Life, ever fresh, ever new, was still going on. My country had survived and was able now to look toward the future.

That was the job for all of us, to rebuild, and I had my part to play in that future by trying to bring my school into being and offer more chances for education to Korean boys.

On our third day in Seoul, Easter Gates arranged through the American Embassy for us to pay a visit to Panmunjom, the historic spot where the treaty was signed that put an end to the Korean War. I had never been there and was eager to make the trip.

First we had to travel through the Demilitarized Zone, a kind of no man's land three miles wide separating North from South Korea and extending for one hundred and fifty miles across the country.

It was a silent and eerie place. Vegetation had taken over the fields; stagnant pools stood in the rice paddies, sprouting with weeds. Wild birds and small animals were everywhere, unmolested in their primitive state; wild flowers bloomed in riotous profusion, unconcerned as to whether they were gazed upon by people or not.

Panmunjom itself is a small cluster of frame buildings perched right on the 38th parallel, which is Korea's counterpart of the Berlin Wall. It is six miles south of Kaesong or Songdo, which had been the capital city long ago in Korea's past, before the Yi Dynasty. More recently, the headquarters of the Southern Methodists in Korea had been located there, up to the time the city was taken over by the Communists.

As we approached Panmunjom, we passed through double lines of barbed wire strung along both sides of the road. We went through gates where sentries stood at attention. We found that our own side of the parallel is supervised by the Swiss and the Swedes, while the North Korean side was guarded by the Czechs and the Poles.

When we reached the center on our side, we were asked to step into the officers' club, a kind of converted barracks resembling a USO canteen. We were served a cold Coca-Cola, then called into a side room and briefed on what we could or should not do when we were finally allowed in the conference room. Above all, we were asked not to use our cameras. By this time, there were about fifty persons in the room. With the exception of the three of us, all were GI's.

We followed our guide, a tall, slim young colonel of the U.S. Eighth Army, into a room which was divided in the middle by a long table. On either side were five chairs.

We were told that the 38th parallel runs down the precise center of the table. When conferences are held to discuss problems common to both North and South—such as water supply —the opposing parties headed by their leaders line up on opposite sides of the table, flanked by newspaper reporters. It is seldom that agreement is reached on any subject of importance. South Korea appears to be much more interested in Panmunjom than North Korea. In the past eight years, for example, we learned that fewer than three hundred visitors had come from the North, while more than thirty thousand had come from the South.

Since there was no conference scheduled to be held on the day of our visit, we decided to cross the 38th parallel and look around on the North Korean side of the DMZ. The first thing we noticed was a Communist guard posted up on top of a hill. He never took his eyes from us wherever we went.

Then we saw ahead of us the fabled "Bridge of No Return,"

which passes from the DMZ into North Korea. A flat wooden structure, it looked so commonplace. Except for the guard posted at either end, it was no different from any other bridge. And yet I knew how impossible it was for anyone to cross over it.

To us from the South, that bridge was symbolic of the curtain of silence that had fallen between North Korea and ourselves. There were so many of our friends and relatives still in the North. What had become of my son-in-law, for example, who had simply vanished one morning and had never been seen since. Was he still alive? How many others whom I had known were still up there? And what was happening to them? Silently I breathed a prayer for those poor people of ours beyond the 38th parallel; I asked God how long we must wait for their release.

After an hour we returned to our own side. The feeling of relief was indescribable. I had known what it was to spend time in prison. But what must it be like, I wondered, to look forward to spending your whole life in a country that had become nothing but one big prison—even though a prison without walls.

The next day I went with my friends to pay a visit to the Orphans' Home. This is a refuge for children run by a friend of mine, Mrs. On Soon Whang. The plight of the children in Korea today is enough to wring one's heart. So many fathers lost their lives in the war that the entire nation has practically become one big orphanage. Fortunately, Mrs. Whang had her Orphans' Home in operation long before the war and thus was ready for the great demands that were made upon it. She and her orphans were flown for safety to the island of Cheju, two hundred and fifty miles off the tip of the Peninsula, at the outbreak of hostilities.

Today, thanks to her own indomitable efforts and those of

her friends in America, Mrs. Whang has built up her orphanage to be the largest in the country where she cares for more than four hundred children at a time. Colonel Dean E. Hess, who wrote *Battle Hymn,* a book based on the war and the orphanage, has been one of Mrs. Whang's most ardent supporters.

We found the children on the playground, lined up according to their ages. The older ones were off working in the fields. The youngest of those present must have been about six. They paid little attention to us, so absorbed were they in the instructions their teachers were giving them.

One of the biggest problems concerning orphans is the fact that although they may be fed, clothed, educated, and cared for, they are still without the greatest essential of all—a mother's love. We were delighted to learn how many of them are receiving attention as individuals through the compassion of the Americans and Canadians who have agreed to become foster parents. In this way, these children who are starved for love can learn what it is to be given affection, even though from a considerable distance.

We found out that day that there are five Korean-American voluntary agencies. They are collectively referred to as KAVA and include: the Christian Children's Fund, Save the Children Federation, World Vision, Foster Parents' Plan, and Swanson Compassion.

Altogether, there were five hundred and fourteen orphanages in Korea in that year of 1961, including fifty homes for babies, accommodating some sixty thousand children. In addition, there were over eight hundred social service centers, some offering clinical services, some caring for waifs and street urchins.

Many of the children at Mrs. Whang's orphanage are gifted, some in music, some in art or in other fields. Mrs. Whang showed us cards that they had painted, depicting everyday scenes in Korean life, such as kite flying, youngsters riding the seesaw, swinging, or washing clothes. On the day of our visit, the children were putting the finishing touches on their handiwork, getting their Christmas cards ready for the annual sale. Their happy faces left a haunting memory. As we drove away I reflected that these children were the innocent victims of war and that it was up to us in the older generation to do as much as we could for them.

We decided to take a day and go have a look at a piece of property owned by the Berea in Korea Foundation which was quite a distance away—about twenty-five miles beyond the city limits of Seoul.

Several years ago I'd come across it while I was searching for a suitable location for the school. I knew this wouldn't do—it was too far out of town for my purposes. But it did embrace three hundred and fifty acres of prime woodland, with many streams and ponds, and I could get it for the modest sum of $2,000. Unable to resist a bargain, I bought it. I am convinced that someday it will prove a valuable asset to the school.

We started out in a jeep on our journey. But even in a jeep we had trouble, because, owing to the rainy season, the road was riddled with potholes and puddles. We came at last to a swollen stream, and unable to go any farther, we had to turn back. We found ourselves on the way to Euijungbu, the place where the North Koreans gathered for their attack on Seoul in 1950.

Ahead of us we saw a group of men in uniform working feverishly. As we drew closer we found they were South Korean and American engineers. A bridge over a swollen stream had been torn away and the engineers were hard at work trying to replace it.

I asked one of them how long he thought it would take. He replied with confidence:

"We should be finished in no more than thirty minutes."

We stood about waiting, watching with admiration while they assembled the new bridge with deftness and skill. Sure enough, in half an hour the bridge was finished and we were able to take to the road again. But it was now too late to reach the property, so we returned to Seoul.

There was just enough time left to pay a visit to the East Gate shopping center. My friends were much interested in Korean handicrafts. My countrymen have preserved the tradition of craftsmanship down through the ages. They have an innate sense of beauty and design which finds expression in brasswork and especially in the unusual lacquer work which is often inlaid with mother-of-pearl. They also do wonderful things in porcelain and in textiles, particularly in embroidered silk.

As I noted the lovely objects displayed for sale, I was impressed by their workmanship. I was convinced that only freedom and faith can release the human potential in the form of imaginative creativity.

The time came all too soon for my companions to return to America. I was glad that it was a clear day with fresh, cool air and blue skies so that they would leave with the happiest possible memory of Korea. I was sorry to see them go. We'd had a marvelous holiday together—one that would stay with us always.

In Seoul, the rest of my summer was crammed full of speaking engagements—luncheons, dinners, and related social events.

My activities gave me the chance to meet Koreans in all walks of life. After having been away such a long time, I was particularly interested in learning what were their most pressing problems. The questions I was asked most often were "How can I earn a living?" and "What is the way out for me?"

This filled me with a great sadness and I tried to get at the core of the problem. It seemed to be twofold, with both aspects closely related.

As was happening all over the world, people were leaving the countryside and crowding into the already swollen cities, looking for employment. The enormous increase in college enrollment was preparing them in greater numbers for positions in the professions, in government or industry which did not exist for them, and at the same time it was giving them a distaste for working with their hands.

What was going to be the solution to all this? Again I was convinced that my school, although it could hardly be expected to make any dent on the total dilemma, was at least a step in the right direction.

Meanwhile, so far as conditions in the country as a whole were concerned, we seemed to have reached a kind of stability.

After the Japanese occupation, which lasted thirty-five years, we Koreans were happy with our Independent Government. The first democratic regime, following Korea's liberation from Japan, was under Dr. Syngman Rhee. It met with disaster in June, 1950, at the hands of the North Korean Communists. The devastation of war bled the people unbearably. But we have survived, and the best is still ahead for us.

Following the heroic action of students against the rigged election of 1960, Dr. Rhee was forced to step down. To be fair, however, it is my opinion that Dr. Rhee will go down in history as one of the great men of Korea. But if that is so, you will ask, why did his government fail? I believe it is because he did not put the right men in the right places. He was surrounded by persons whom he trusted, but who were greedy for position and money. Some became millionaires almost overnight. Among his achievements, he should be credited with the building of a strong Republic of Korea (R.O.K.) Army of six hundred thousand well-trained men. Korea has one of the largest standing armies in the free world. And how he was hated by the Communists for this accomplishment!

I found that industry was expanding rapidly. I had the opportunity to visit a flat glass factory which had been built recently at Inchon. It was exciting to watch sand being converted into glass. Korea, being a peninsula, has endless sandy beaches, and since the principal ingredient in the making of glass is sand, glassmaking is a "natural" Korean industry.

Both men and women were working in the factory, and they all appeared to be very proud of their achievements. It was noontime, and the shift taking an hour for lunch and rest came to the chapel to hear me speak. I told them how privileged I thought they were to be taking part in the building of a new Korea. I pointed out to them that the strength of the new nation depended upon them. Their efforts, only, could bring about the revitalization of industry, agriculture, and mining, as well as the development of all the natural resources.

The director of the glass factory drove us to the park where a statue of General MacArthur stood. He is well-remembered for his brilliantly conceived landing behind enemy lines at Inchon. The landing took place on September 18, 1950, and was the turning point of the war, leading to the victory of the United Nations forces.

Although my sight-seeing activities were most pleasant, my primary purpose for being in Korea was to obtain a site for my school—and find it I would.

For sixty-three days, I spent every free minute I had looking for a possible location. But all real estate within reach of Seoul was so fabulously expensive that I began to wonder whether I would ever get what I wanted.

Then one morning, with only a few days left before I had to return to the States, a broker took me up on a small rise of ground about eight miles out of town. With a gesture of his pipe and a thrust of his chin, he indicated a hilly area about two miles away.

I did not know that any piece of land so incredibly wild could still exist this close to the city. The reason we had to scrutinize the property from such a distance, the broker explained, was because this was as near as we could get. There was no access road!

The place appeared to be a jumble of rocks and pine trees, of hills and orchards, and sloping fields. Mountains could be seen in the distance. Nearby was a pleasant valley with a stream flowing through it. It looked delightful.

One thing puzzled me.

"Those tall white things sticking up," I said to the broker. "What are those?"

"Oh, stones," he replied casually.

"What kind of stones?" I persisted.

"Oh, gravestones, I guess." In an offhand manner, he added, "It seems to me I remember hearing that some generals were buried there."

"How many?"

"Oh, not many. Maybe a dozen or so."

I did not find this piece of information disturbing. My woman's instinct told me clearly that this was the place I had been looking for and that I was not likely to find another one like it. I did not intend to let a few long-dead generals get in my way.

I was in no mood to think about any drawbacks. I did not even stop to consider exactly how many acres the broker was including in the gesture of his pipe and the thrust of his chin.

That night, back in Seoul, as I reviewed the day's experience, I knew that was the property I wanted. In the next few days I talked it over with my friends. They tried to discourage me, telling me that they thought my choice of a location was totally unwise.

But I made up my mind that I was going to become the owner of that land before I left Korea. I opened negotiations. The present owner must have sensed how badly I wanted it, for it seemed to me that the price he put on it was not only high, but exorbitant. The day came when I was to take off for America, September 1, 1961, and the matter had not yet been settled. My plane was due to leave at 3:00 P.M., which meant that I would have to leave my hotel at 1:00 P.M. in order to catch the bus for the airport. That also meant that the owner and I had only until noon, at the latest, to come to an agreement.

The property owner was to come to see me at 9:00 A.M., which should have given us sufficient time. But for some reason he was an hour and a half late; therefore, we did not begin our negotiations until around half past ten.

We opened with a deadlock. Our ideas on price were quite far apart, and there seemed to be no prospect whatever of our drawing any closer.

After we had argued for a while, I happened to look out the window. The rain was coming down in buckets. The seller stated his minimum and I stated my maximum. We were still poles apart. I listened to the rain drumming on the roof and wondered whether my plane would be able to take off. At length, the owner stated bluntly that either he would get his price or there would be no deal. Between moments of dickering I prayed silently to God that He might show me some way to come to an agreement.

Presently someone came in with the word that my plane had been unable to land and had turned back to Tokyo. Immediately the pressure caused by my approaching departure seemed to be relieved. No one wanted to go out into that pouring rain, so there was nothing to do but continue with our negotiations.

At this point the broker took a firmer hand in the situation. He initiated a series of adroit maneuvers, first suggesting that I be prepared to give a little more, to which I agreed. Then he suggested that the owner accept a little less. Thus, step by step, he brought us closer together. By one o'clock, we had reached a point where we were ready to sign the contract. We got out our pens and, with appropriate flourishes, put our names to the document that gave me title to the land.

I looked up for the first time in over an hour. The rain had stopped; the sky was clearing.

A few minutes later I received word that a Civilian Air Transport plane would be leaving for Tokyo that evening at seven. I made arrangements to be on it.

The plane had been scheduled originally to take off that morning. But owing to the rain its departure had been delayed until evening. Once more I had proof that God's intervention is not to be doubted. Again and again I have been shown evidence that His help is there when I have need of it.

When I was driven to the airport that afternoon, the sun was shining. Blue sky began to peep out between cottony white clouds; the new-washed fields were fresh and green; the whole world was shining. All of this seemed like the best possible omen for my return to the United States.

I confidently promised the friends who had come to see me off that I would be back the following year. I had no doubt now that I would be able to raise the money for my school.

8

*

Blueprint for a Dream

WHEN I WAS BACK in the United States, I hardly took the time to unpack before I hurried to the bank to have a look at my balance.

"What balance?" I might have said. It was painfully close to zero.

But at any rate I was the owner of property. I could actually start to build my school any day now. That is, *if* I could lay hands on the money. "Oh, well," I said to myself, "nothing is impossible. I might as well get started."

I took to the road again, delivering my lectures, and before long I was able to make some deposits. They were small ones, but they made me feel I had at least made a beginning.

Then one morning, I received a letter from a practical-minded friend of mine in Seoul. He told me that for my sake, he had taken a day off and had gone out to have a good look at my property. To reach it, he explained, he had to walk cross country. He wasn't content to have a look at it from two miles away as I had done. Then he went on to say,

"Well, Induk, I've gone over every inch of the property you've bought. All I can say is that it hurts me to see you throw your money away on a tract so utterly worthless. Only a crazy woman would buy such a place."

He pointed out to me, without mincing any words, that the twenty-five or so acres I had bought were, to say the least, totally impractical. There was no road—this, of course, was no surprise to me. But when I saw this information before me in his "voice-of-doom" letter, the land suddenly seemed much more inaccessible than it had when I gazed upon it from across the valley. He gleefully pointed out that there was no power line anywhere near and that all electricity would have to be brought in; there was no water and in one part a high hill cut off the nicest view.

The worst, however, was yet to come.

"I feel I must also tell you about the cemetery. On one corner of your land is quite a large graveyard (pictures enclosed). I should say that it must contain about five hundred graves. A number of them are marked with rather heavy stones, some of which would appear to weigh as much as one ton each."

A groan escaped me as I read.

"I do not know whether the government will allow you to move the graves. Even if it is possible from a legal standpoint, the job itself is going to cost you a small fortune. However, that is your problem."

I could see him writing this dutiful letter, self-righteously washing his hands of the whole matter. His words stung me. I felt that they made me look foolish, and I don't like to look foolish.

My cheeks burning with anger, I sat down and wrote my reply:

"Very well, then. We will build a road. We will bring in electricity. We will dig a well. We will level the hill. And we will even move the graves. Then, surely, there will be nothing to complain about."

Having said it—I had to believe it.

Eight months later I returned to Korea, eager to see my property. I visited the real estate broker and chided him for not having made clear to me just how many graves there were on my land.

He merely shrugged his shoulders, grinned at me, and said, "If I had told you the truth about the property you never would have bought it. But I knew that piece of land would be the best one you could possibly get for your school. So, you see, I have really done you a big favor."

I could not disagree with him. He was so right.

Finally, I found myself on the site for the school, a site that the Berea in Korea Foundation actually owned—almost thirty acres of it—on the outskirts of Seoul. I could hardly believe it was true.

And what a magnificent location it was! My heart purred with pride. Off to the northwest I could see clearly Sam Kok San, the famous Three-Horned Mountain, now turning purple in the afternoon sun. In another direction lay Nam San, Seoul's South Mountain. At my feet was a lovely, wide and winding stream. As a challenge, across the valley were the handsome modern buildings of Seoul College of Technology, known as Korea's M.I.T.

The shrill toot of a train whistle split the afternoon stillness, drawing my attention to the railroad tracks passing to the northeast of the property. This was an important feature of our location, for it would make it easy for the boys to get back and forth to Seoul.

I looked back at the property itself. I suppressed a sigh as I thought how much remained to be done—land to be cleared, a road to be built, wells to be drilled, and electricity to be brought in.

But there were even more difficult tasks facing us. The

graveyard was there all right; and it would have to be moved.

And that hill behind? Surely that must go. Where it stood was the perfect spot for an athletic field. But it would take weeks of labor and quantities of money which I did not have.

My eye turned back to the view across the valley. Just ahead lay a series of low hills, rising and falling like the humps of a dragon.

I was reminded of my birth sign—the Day of the Dragon. Now when the tiger sees his prey, he pounces. But when the dragon makes up his mind on his objective, he moves slowly, steadily, indomitably. Nothing can stand in his way. I would emulate the dragon—except that I could not move too slowly; there was no time.

My first job was to seek out an architect. Before I could make my dream become a fact, I had to have a blueprint for it. I had to get everything down in black and white—or rather, blue and white. A young man had been recommended to me who was not as yet well known, but who had remarkable talent. His name was Sang Chin La, and he had helped to design the beautiful resort for GI's, "Walker Hill," as a memorial to General Walton H. Walker, who died in the Korean War.

I invited the youthful architect to have dinner with me at Korea House, a restaurant in Seoul famous for its native dishes, and operated by a woman friend of mine.

In Korea we often meet at tea houses or restaurants to discuss our business because we seldom have any room in our homes which is appropriate for such occasions.

Sitting across the table from Sang Chin, I said, "I have no wish to pose as an expert. I will leave the details to you. But I will try to give you an idea of the feelings I want to express.

"The buildings should be in harmony with their setting; I am anxious above all for them to convey an atmosphere of simplicity, sincerity, and serenity.

"I want everything to be in proportion. Too often I have

seen a building with its roof hanging too far down, so that it looked like a child in an oversized hat."

I explained to him that we wanted our buildings to be an example of good taste to our young students, ones that they would remember and that would inspire them when it came time for them to build homes of their own.

Sang Chin had a dreamy, faraway look. But he nodded and smiled as I spoke and made little jottings with his pencil. I felt quite certain that he had grasped what I was trying to convey.

I was absorbed in the exciting business of planning as the blueprints were drawn up, and at the same time I had to plow my way through the tedious details of setting up an Auxiliary Foundation. This was necessary to meet the requirements of the Ministry of Education.

There were forms to be filled out, interviews to be held, papers to be signed. I did not enjoy it, but it had to be done. All in all, the cumbersome business took me exactly fifty-three days. At about this time, as I was reliving my experience, a strange thought came to me.

The revolution that broke out on the day of my departure from the United States, which would have kept me from going to Korea at all if I had listened to the advice of well-meaning friends, had turned out to be a blessing in disguise.

This is the way everything worked out:

They had a saying in Korea which went, "Everything is possible under the Syngman Rhee regime; at the same time everything is impossible." This meant you could get anything done if you had the money, but nothing would happen if you had no cash. The regime of Dr. John M. Chang didn't last long enough to bring about any great change.

But when General Chung Hee Park's government came to power, profound changes took place very quickly. Before that time, one of my friends said, "I scarcely dare to go out by my-

self because of the pickpockets in the daytime and the hood-
lums after dark." Now the deplorable conditions in the cities
were rapidly rectified by the new government. The criminals
were taken off the streets and sent to rehabilitation work camps
something like the Civilian Conservation Corps (C.C.C.)
camps in the United States during the war.

The new regime was anxious to enjoy a good reputation.
For that reason, its representatives were much more sympathetic to a project such as my proposed school than the Syngman Rhee government would have been. They did everything
possible to cut the red tape. As so often happens in life, what
appeared at first to be a disaster turned out to be quite the
opposite.

Finally, I had done all I could in Korea on this visit, and the
time came for me to return to the United States. Now I had to
raise the necessary funds to turn the blueprints into actual
buildings in order to bring Induk Vocational School into
being and enable it to live up to its exciting potential in that
beautiful setting.

The time drew near for my departure. I was feeling somewhat sad at leaving these familiar surroundings, so on two
successive evenings friends persuaded me to see two Korean
movies which had been released recently. Both were based on
well-known historical novels with which every Korean,
whether young or old, is well acquainted. Since both stories
are classics which have been tested by time, they tell us something about the nature and character of the Korean people.

The first is a love story, concerning the forbidden romance
between Choon Hyang (Spring Fragrance), a beautiful
maiden who is the daughter of a former dancing girl, and Yi
Do Ryung, the handsome son of the local magistrate.

From his vantage point in a distant pavilion, Yi Do Ryung
sees Choon Hyang swinging in her garden. He falls in love at
the first sight of her. But he cannot ask her to marry him for

two reasons: He is still studying for his future career, and his family would not grant permission for him to marry the daughter of a dancing girl. However, he makes up his mind that he will have her. One night he climbs up the high wall surrounding her house and goes to her room, where an oil lamp is burning low.

Yi Do Ryung says, "I was brave when I climbed up the wall, but when I held the handle of the door to her room in my hand, I became weak. . . . Yes, I was too weak to open it. I trembled. . . ."

Yi Do Ryung woos Choon Hyang. They marry secretly and Yi Do Ryung does not tell his family. In time Yi Do Ryung's father must move to another town. The bridegroom is parted from his wife because he is dependent upon his father for support.

A new magistrate comes to the village to take the father's place. The successor is a wicked and lustful man. Upon seeing the young and beautiful Choon Hyang, he is taken with her at once and desires her for his concubine. Again and again he presses his suit; again and again she refuses. But the magistrate is persistent and demands that she yield to him. If she does not give in, he informs her, she will be tortured and thrown into prison. Choon Hyang would rather die than become a concubine while still married to Yi Do Ryung. Time passes and she hears no word from her husband. Still she does not yield and the magistrate makes good his threat.

At long last, Yi Do Ryung returns to his home village. He is traveling incognito, for he comes as a Royal inspector, secretly sent to investigate the new magistrate's rule. Yi Do Ryung quickly discovers the wrong that has been done Choon Hyang because she has remained faithful to him, and he releases not only his wife, but all the other innocents who have been victims of the magistrate's whims. He orders the wicked magistrate to be punished.

Choon Hyang and Yi Do Ryung live together happily

thereafter. They became renowned symbols of romance and fidelity, like Romeo and Juliet in the Western world.

The other movie is the story of a lovely young girl named Sim Chung who sells herself for the sake of her poor blind father in order that his sight may be restored.

Sim Chung's mother had died when she was seven days old. The blind father raises the child by begging mother's milk from different women. He carries his little daughter in one arm while tapping his way with a cane held in his other hand.

When Sim Chung is old enough to know the thoughtfulness and self-sacrifice with which her father has brought her up, she prays to Buddha for the restoration of his eyesight. In her prayers she pleads, "God made the sun and moon to be seen with man's eyes. If my father has lost his sight because of any mistake he made in the past, let me pay for it with my life and give him back his sight."

One day some time afterward, a Buddhist priest comes to her village. He says, "If you could give an offering of three hundred bushels of rice to Buddha, your father's sight would be restored." But it is not in any way possible for Sim Chung to obtain so large a quantity of rice.

Soon after the priest's visit, a group of traders who have come from a distant place make their way through the village, looking for a pure girl of fifteen years of age to be offered as a human sacrifice for the success of their journey. During the remainder of their sojourn they will have to pass over the most dangerous waterway of the sea. If they can bury a girl alive in the ocean as an offering to the Dragon, they have been told, they will enjoy a safe voyage and their businesses will prosper.

Sim Chung meets the traders and relates her life's wish for her father. She asks, "Could you buy me for three hundred bushels of rice? I am a girl of the right age and qualifications that you are searching for."

They take pity on her and buy her for the price she has set.

Three hundred bushels of rice are sent at once to the Temple as an offering to Buddha in the hope that Sim Chung's father will have his sight restored. Sim Chung starts to prepare herself as a sacrifice to the God of the Sea for the merchants. She is to depart with them on the fifteenth day of the following month. In her last days she cooks especially delicious meals for her father and helps guide the chopsticks to his lips. She washes his clothes and mends them and prepares for spring, summer, and fall, as well as winter. While she is sewing on his garments, away into the night, she thinks about her father and his handicap. She wonders how in the world he will be able to live without her. And she weeps; but she weeps silently, for fear of waking him.

Finally, her last evening comes. She stays up all that night before finishing the chores at hand. As the sky grows pale, the cock starts to crow. She cries, "Cock, cock, don't you crow! If you crow it will mean that it is dawn. If it is dawn then it is the day I will have to die." She thinks sadly to herself, "An arrow already shot and lost, and the water already poured and spilled . . ."

The dawn arrives; the traders come and stand outside the house, impatient to take her away. Sim Chung begs them to wait until she cooks one last breakfast for her father. When he has finished eating, she reveals to him what she has done. Her poor father is stunned. He cries out, "But I would rather have you and be blind than to lose you and have my sight!"

Sim Chung is deeply moved but knows that she must keep her end of the bargain, and so she parts from her father.

The ship sails and Sim Chung is thrown into the sea to appease the Dragon's wrath. But as soon as she sinks beneath the waves, she is taken into the Dragon's palace. The king and queen of the sea, moved by her great beauty of spirit, do not kill her but instead make her a princess. In time they give a great feast to which they invite all the beggars, the lame, and the blind from the land above. Toward the end of the feast, Sim Chung looks down the table; she cries out with delight. There, enjoying the banquet, she recognizes her own blind father. When the father hears his daughter's voice, his eyes open and he can see! For the first time he gazes upon her beauty. And as Choon Hyang became known as the most loyal wife in all of Korea, Sim Chung gained renown as the most filial daughter in the land!

I went out of the movie theater into the starry night, feeling uplifted and inspired. The two films, coming one after the other, were a timely reminder of the spirit of my people, of their courage, their steadfastness, and their loyalty.

Like so many things in my life, this experience had come to me just when I needed it most. My countrymen were indeed deserving of the best I could do for them. I rededicated myself to their service.

What did it matter that just to purchase the site and draw the blueprints had eaten up every cent I possessed? I still had my faith in God and in my friends in the United States and Canada.

9

*

"But Go Ahead!"

IT IS CURIOUS how one's spirits can rise or fall with a change in environment.

When I was in Seoul the prospects of all the money I had to raise and of the obstacles that loomed ahead did not depress me in the least. I felt completely equal to the task at hand.

But when I found myself back in Washington, D.C., with the job staring me in the face, I must say that my courage dwindled. It was like arriving at the base of a mountain you have already agreed to climb, looking upward for the first time, and becoming aware of just how high it is.

My concerns, however, were overshadowed by an event of great importance. Iris had been invited to give her graduation organ recital in the great and magnificent Washington Cathedral. How proud she had made me. My daughter had been chosen to play that organ, which is certainly one of the most beautiful in the country. And she was the first Korean ever to give an organ recital in America.

Those few days that remained before the Sunday of the

recital were hectic ones indeed, with visits to the hairdresser, last-minute run-throughs, and a steady succession of phone calls.

But the great day came at last, sunny and beautiful, and we were on our way up Massachusetts Avenue to the cathedral. Iris and I separated at the front door. I took her two boys to find a seat where we could see as well as hear, while Iris went around to the rear entrance to make her way to the organ loft.

I chatted with friends a while, and one of them mentioned that Woodrow Wilson was buried in the cathedral. His name had always meant much to me because of his Fourteen Points program and his support of small nations' rights.

We took our seats and then Iris appeared, wearing a bright red brocaded Korean blouse and skirt. I could see her bending over, kicking off her high-heeled shoes in order to put on her narrow flat-heeled ones, the better to manipulate the organ pedals.

I could only think how tiny she looked seated there, her dress a small spot of bright color against the background of those huge pipes. All around me were our friends, the friends of years' standing, some of whom had traveled hundreds of miles just to hear Iris play.

And then her fingers touched the keys. Immediately the vaulted stone rafters of the huge cathedral thundered and echoed to the majestic chords of Bach. Chills ran up and down my spine. There was no doubt as to her mastery of the instrument.

What a thrilling moment that was in my life! What a reward for all we had both endured. How good God had been to us. And then I forgot that it was Iris who was playing. The music entered my soul. My thoughts soared and traveled far away.

Woodrow Wilson was buried here—the only president whose resting place is in the city of Washington, D.C. As I sat listening to Bach, what memories the sound of that name stirred in my mind. All at once I was transported to quite a different setting—to a cold, dark, airless prison cell.

It was the year 1919, not long after the Paris Peace Conference that ended World War I. I was being held by the Japanese in Seoul's Westgate Prison for my part in the 1919 Korean Independence Movement.

My life was miserable in the extreme. I had been thrown into solitary confinement. The cell was damp with the chill of winter. It had no window. My ration of boiled soybeans served three times a day was barely sufficient to sustain life. An old blouse, trousers, and skirt were all the clothing I had. I had no hope of ever getting out of there.

And then one day, a prison guard, who happened to be a loyal Korean, passed the door to my cell and whispered two words:

"Woodrow Wilson!"

Woodrow Wilson. That's all—nothing more. He left me puzzling over his utterance. I could not for the life of me grasp its significance. For the next few days and nights the sound of that name sustained me. I repeated it over and over to myself as I fell asleep after having said my prayers.

Then one day I received a package from the outside. It was a cardboard box containing a dress. I examined the dress carefully, for that was one of the ways in which secret messages were smuggled in to us.

Sure enough! I found a carefully hidden note. With trembling hands I took the barely legible paper, with its writing in Hangul, to the stream of pale light that filtered in through the bars of the prison door. Again, that name, this time spelled out phonetically in Korean characters—Woodrow Wilson!

Then I read the message:

"Woodrow Wilson is coming to Korea. Hope! Hang on! Liberation is at hand!"

That's all there was. But it was all I needed. I let my imagination play with it. My hopes fed on it.

I already had heard that President Wilson and the president of our country, Syngman Rhee, had been close friends ever since Mr. Rhee had been a student at Princeton when Woodrow Wilson was president of that institution. I knew that at this moment President Wilson was perhaps the most powerful person in the entire world.

It was quite within the realm of possibility that if he were planning to come to Korea, it could mean the liberation of our country from the Japanese yoke. And the immediate result, even before his arrival, could well be the freeing of the imprisoned Korean patriots.

That night after inspection was over, I lay down on the floor next to the rathole in the wall. I whispered to my fellow prisoner, a woman who was also in solitary, in the next cell to me,

"Woodrow Wilson is coming! He is coming to Seoul to meet with Syngman Rhee!"

The word spread like wildfire from cell to cell.

Hope! Now we had hope! Life had some meaning again. There was something to look forward to. Hope is to the spirit what oxygen is to the body. It sustains life. How great are those words of the Bible—faith, hope, and love—in recognizing the three cornerstones of human existence.

In the light of what we now knew, we read into every sound, every action, every chance remark of the guards some reassuring significance.

Woodrow Wilson would come to see our plight for himself—and then we would soon be set free.

Of course Woodrow Wilson never did come to Korea to visit Syngman Rhee. This information had proved to be just another one of those wild rumors that circulated in the prison from time to time for no apparent reason. But untrue though it was, it served to keep our spirits up through a particularly trying time. We were liberated not long afterward, although for an altogether different reason.

So you can see what a very special meaning the name of Woodrow Wilson has always had for me.

And here I was, forty-three years later, sitting in the very cathedral where the great American president was buried. And my daughter's playing of Bach was so powerful that my thoughts leaped back to the past, to the days of my ordeal and to a whispered name that did so much to help me survive my experience.

I thought about all our lives and of the thread of continuity that runs through them unseen, so strongly affecting them, linking them one to the other. And I saw Woodrow Wilson's unwitting effect on my destiny as a part of that continuity.

Then I thought of my mother and the lonely years she spent as a wandering peddler, undertaking her exile cheerfully so long as I might have my education which would give me a man's chance in the world. I thought how her great-hearted sacrifice and cheerful good sense had inspired not only me and my work, but my daughter Iris and her work; how it would ultimately result in bringing the benefits of education to some unknown Korean boy still unaware of what was in store for him.

My doubts fell away from me like veils of mist. My spirits soared with the great soaring chords of Bach's thunder. God would not let me down.

I walked out of the cathedral into the tranquil sunshine of a Washington Sunday afternoon with a firm step that reflected my firmness of purpose.

Through a strange arrangement of circumstances, I had been granted a vision of the warp and woof woven by the threads of life, of its pattern, its mystery, and its meaning.

Yes, there was a purpose to it all, a purpose which could be realized through strength rooted in faith.

I was no longer assailed by fears. I would raise that money; I would find it somehow. My dream *would* come into being!

The work would go on.

One night while I was riding along in a Greyhound, thinking about building my school, I recalled a scrap of conversation from the past. A woman was introduced to me after a church meeting in Michigan where I had been speaking. She seemed keenly interested by my account of what I was doing. We talked for a while and then she said, "Oh, I would love to have you meet some friends of mine, Dorothy and Stanley Kresge. They do such wonderful things to help people. I want them to hear about your work."

At that time I was in no position to take advantage of her offer. It was too bad, but my dream was still in the embryo stage. I had nothing on paper that I could show to anyone.

Now that I thought of it, my situation was entirely changed. I had the blueprints and I owned the land. Perhaps it was a good thing that I hadn't been ready before; my need for funds was now much greater. I decided to write to my friend at once and ask her for an introduction to the Kresges.

Happily, she complied with my request immediately. The appointment with Mr. Kresge was set for eleven o'clock on the morning of November 13.

All through my life the number 13 has had a special, and beneficial, significance in my affairs. It was on the 13th of September that I arrived at Wesleyan College in Macon, Georgia, to begin my schooling in the United States. It was on the 13th of March that I set foot for the first time in Canada. Now, once more, this meeting which could have such importance in my work was scheduled for the 13th. I felt it must be a good omen.

My spirits were high as I stepped off the bus in Detroit. November weather in Michigan can be depressing. But this morning the air was bright and full of sparkle, the city washed with sunshine. I sought out the building where the Kresge Foundation had its offices.

Suddenly an eerie feeling came over me. The neighborhood had an air of familiarity about it. I seemed to know it. I felt almost as though I had seen it in a dream—or that I had been here in a former incarnation.

The large white building across the street, for example. Surely I had seen it before. And then I noticed the sign, "Masonic Temple."

I had indeed been here before—thirty-four years ago! It was inside that auditorium, from its platform, that I had given my maiden speech before a large audience.

For a moment I closed my eyes and lived the scene once more: remembering the frightened young woman who was myself; the microphone that had to be lowered especially for me; the endless sea of faces stretching out to the distant walls; the returning echo of my own voice; and finally the growing confidence and exhilaration, as I felt that electric current of oneness with my audience. Then and there I had received my baptism as a public speaker.

Yes, thirty-four years had passed since that memorable night. And not long afterward. Dr. Hutchins had given me his exciting idea for "Berea in Korea." My spirits sank for the moment as I reviewed in my mind the long years of work and struggle and single-minded concentration, of heartbreak and setback and disappointment and frustration. I do not want to leave the impression that I was feeling sorry for myself, however. All through those years I'd had a wonderful time. The only thing that bothered me was that so many years had passed and I'd not yet been able to build my school—my dream had not yet come true.

Still, I did have the blueprints! And I had the location—the hilltop from which I could look the Three-Horned Mountain squarely in the eye. Perhaps fulfillment was at hand!

Anyway, I was a tiger! With renewed courage, I went on to find Mr. Kresge. But in spite of all my efforts to prepare myself psychologically for the meeting, the encounter took me completely by surprise.

I was about to ask for him at the reception desk in the lobby when a tall, well-groomed man with a friendly manner stepped up to me, and said, "Excuse me, are you Mrs. Pahk?"

I said that I was.

"I am Stanley Kresge," he replied. "Shall we go up to my office?"

Mr. Kresge put me immediately at ease. After we were comfortably seated and the preliminary remarks disposed of, I unfolded my plan. When I thought I had captured his interest, I brought out our set of blueprints for the school and spread them before him on the desk.

Mr. Kresge listened courteously, occasionally interrupting to ask a question or make a comment. But I could not get any clue from what he said as to what he was really thinking.

I took heart when, at one point in the conversation, he said,

"Do you happen to know Dorothy Jhung?"

"Yes I do!" I exclaimed. "She is a very dear friend of mine." Mrs. Jhung had been close to me for much of my life. She had attended Ewha College in the class just two years ahead of mine. She had been one of the first three Korean girls to be graduated from there.

We were both surprised to learn that we had another friend in common, besides the one who had brought us together. We went on talking for half an hour or more. When it came time to go, Mr. Kresge suggested that I put in writing everything I had told him about the school so that he could discuss it with

the other members of his board. At the same time he took
pains to make it clear that he was not actually promising me
any assistance. In spite of his cautionary observation, I could
not help feeling that he was going to help me. Otherwise, why
would God have brought us together?

I left Mr. Kresge's office that morning with a full heart. But
my pockets were still empty.

I had not hesitated to ask Mr. Kresge for assistance because
of something my mother had once told me. She said,

"Never ask anyone to help you to do anything you are not
willing to do yourself. Do you want someone to give to a
cause? Then give yourself before you ask anyone else to
do likewise."

After all, I had raised most of the money for "Berea in
Korea" by my own efforts. Also, I felt sure there was a chance
that Mr. Kresge would help us because I did not think such a
busy man would be likely to take half an hour out of his
crowded day unless he was interested.

When I got back to the house where I was staying in Detroit, I found a letter from Nam Kyu Chung, my nephew in
Korea. I opened it eagerly, hoping that it contained good
news. I was taken aback, therefore, when I read, ". . . Building
materials are getting scarcer by the minute. We must order
them right now if we are not to be caught short. Remember, in
this situation of scarcity, anyone who is able to make a sub-
stantial down payment will have priority in getting supplies. It
will be necessary for you to send me quite a large sum of
money at once, if we are to keep to your construction timetable."

Here was a new dilemma facing me. In order to understand
it, the reader must know something of the difference between
building procedures in Korea and the United States. In Korea,
we cannot afford any waste, so before we start to build, we
must calculate all the materials that are going to be needed,

down to the last brick, the last piece of hardware, the last bag of cement.

I sat down with my No. 2 yellow pencil and began to total up my assets. This is what I found:

In some respects the outlook was favorable. This was the best time of year from the standpoint of raising money. It would soon be time to send out my annual Christmas appeal. I was booked solidly for lectures every night of the week—Saturday excepted—from November through March. Last reports from the publisher indicated that my book, *September Monkey*, was still selling very well. From all these sources, the sum total of my personal efforts. I might realize as much as $13,000.

Then there were the buildings owned by the Berea in Korea Foundation, in Washington, D.C. If I were to sell these I might realize as much as $35,000. Also I had another $10,000 in cash, given me only last year by a friend in Ohio which I had been saving for just such an emergency. All in all, my potential resources added up to $60,000.

But then—jumping over to the other side of the ledger and looking facts in the face—my No. 2 yellow pencil had bad news for me. Just to get the building up on a minimum basis, without any trimmings, was going to cost us $85,000. In other words, the pencil showed me clearly, we were $25,000 short.

Oh, but wait a minute. The honest yellow pencil reminded me that I was $6,000 in debt. That brought the amount of my deficit up to $31,000!

What to do? What to do?

I could use the $10,000 to make the down payment necessary for obtaining the needed materials. But wasn't this taking too long a chance when I did not have the money in sight to assure the school's completion?

On the other hand, if I did not take the chance, the materials would undoubtedly slip away from me and I might never have the opportunity to buy them again at a price I could afford.

Besides, if I lost my nerve and didn't go ahead, would God still believe in me?

I took a deep breath, went to the telephone, and sent the following reply to my nephew:

"Cabling you ten thousand dollars. Go ahead. Schedule ground-breaking ceremony for Easter Sunday."

Having reached my decision, I proceeded to concentrate all my energies on trying to earn money, which helped push my concern over financing the school to the back of my mind.

First I got busy and wrote out my Christmas appeal. Then I went on with my lectures. Back and forth across the continent I rode all that winter, through blizzards and below-zero cold.

I ended my engagements only when the time drew near for me to go to Korea for the ground-breaking ceremonies.

When I added up the income from my winter's endeavors it came to $13,000—almost to the penny what my No. 2 yellow pencil had told me that I could expect.

10

*

"I? An International Gambler?"

THE GROUND-BREAKING CEREMONIES for the school had been set for Easter Sunday of 1963. By this time I was back in Seoul. When I awoke Easter morning at the home of a friend in Pildong, a residential section of Seoul, I looked out the window onto a rainy gray world.

And this was the day we had chosen for the ceremonies. They were to take place at 4:00 P.M., the Hour of the Monkey.

We had chosen Easter Sunday for a very special reason. We wanted to honor the memory of two Christian missionaries, Henry G. Appenzeller, the Methodist, and Horace G. Underwood, the Presbyterian, who had both played such significant roles in the modernization of Korea.

By a strange coincidence both men had arrived on the same boat at Inchon on Easter Sunday, in the year 1885. This was three years after Korea, then known as the "Hermit Kingdom" because of its long history of isolation, had signed its first treaty of friendship with the United States.

As I lay back in bed, trying to swallow my disappointment

over the weather, my thoughts turned to these two men. I recalled how much they had done for Korea, and for Korean women in particular.

Until their arrival, there were no schools for girls. Females were not considered sufficiently intelligent to be worth educating. The two men came bringing with them the firm conviction that all Koreans, men and women alike, should have the opportunity of receiving an education. The missionaries who followed soon after them continued this tradition and many Christian schools were founded which were attended by an increasing number of Korean women each year.

Indeed, I myself, owed my education to the Methodist missionaries, for I had received my early training at the Ewha High School and College (now Ewha Woman's University) in Seoul, which was the first school for girls in Korea.

As I lay there waiting for the rain to let up, I blessed the memory of Henry Appenzeller. Then I fell to wondering how many Americans know, as we Koreans do, the circumstances of his death which made him an everlasting hero to us.

Dr. Appenzeller was on his way from his home in Seoul to attend a meeting of the Bible Translation committee at Chemulpo, now called Inchon. On the same boat was a girl student from Ewha School returning home alone for a vacation. Dr. Appenzeller, finding this out, took her under his wing. As they neared shore the steamer on which they were traveling collided with another ship in the fog. Dr. Appenzeller was on deck at the time. The minute he felt the shuddering crash, he thought of the girl student helpless in her stateroom below decks. Immediately, he went to the rescue.

Whether he found her or not, no one knows. By that time the ship was sinking, and it was too late for Dr. Appenzeller to save himself. In my country we have not forgotten the missionary who gave his own life for a Korean girl.

The morning wore on. But the rain only came down harder. Friends began calling me on the telephone.

"Do you intend to go ahead with the ceremony?" they asked me. "Don't you think it would be more sensible to cancel it? There's still time, you know."

"Certainly I'm not going to cancel it!" I told everyone who called. "The weather will be clear by noon."

The rain did finally let up. But the sky remained overcast and threatening, as though it might unloose a downpour at any moment. Still, I would not cancel.

Around noon, my nephew, Nam Kyu Chung, came for me in a taxi, and we drove out to the school site. For a time it looked as though we might be the only ones who were going to come. But my faith remained unshaken. On this great day, nothing could go wrong.

And then, sure enough, I looked up to see some sixty of my friends coming on foot along the muddy road. It gave me a thrill when I recognized among them the benign face of the Rev. Chai Hee Um, who had consented to officiate at the ceremonies.

The Rev. Mr. Um had always meant something special to me. He had conducted the funeral service for my mother several years before. He had followed my career—consoling, inspiring, and encouraging me.

The time had come.

As the photographers trained their cameras on me, I dug the spade in and lifted the first shovelful of earth. It flew through the air, and through the shower of dirt I could see the flags of the school fluttering in the breeze. The ceremonies ended. We were on our way.

Now, the long, hard job, first of bringing the school into being, then of making it a success, loomed ahead.

But first things first. The initial step was to put in a good solid foundation. I have learned from my Christian faith that one can do well in life only when there is a dependable base on which to build. A bricklayer had once pointed out to me that he was always especially careful with the foundation, because as his wall rose, even the tiniest mistake became multiplied many times.

I spent long hours discussing the project with the various contractors whom I had come to know and respect. In the end I decided to supervise the undertaking myself. Can you imagine the nerve it took for a woman, with no experience in this sort of work, to assume responsibility for a man's job? Well, I made up my mind to do it.

I never could have done it without the help of my nephew, who was the son of my former sister-in-law. I had been able to help him get an education by obtaining a scholarship for him awarded by a woman whom I had never met. He had majored in economics but his talents lay in other directions. He was a born engineer. This job would have been complicated even for a more experienced man, but I had complete confidence in his ability to handle it.

Nam Kyu Chung had always been fascinated by construction. Fortunately, he had already demonstrated that he had common sense, and friendly contractors had tested him, reporting that they thought he would be able to fill in for me very well when I was away.

First we had to build a road wide enough to carry all the necessary materials into the property. Difficult as it was, we accomplished this without incident. Then we encountered our first big obstacle. We were simply going to have to move that graveyard. With government consent we had already moved and reburied the dead. But the tombstones presented a real problem.

The upright tombstones themselves were not so difficult. They were tall and carried inscriptions to the dead. Sometimes they also had statues to indicate whether the deceased was a scholar, a nobleman, or a soldier. But the biggest obstacle lay in moving the large block of granite, a kind of table, which stood in front of each family plot.

Once a year on August 15, by the lunar calendar, the living relatives gathered to hold a feast, paying tribute to the ancestors. At other times they would pay special tribute to the members of their immediate family on the day they had died. These special observances would be kept up for a matter of three years, after which those who had been honored would pass into the realm of the general ancestors.

These granite blocks appeared almost impossible to move, for some of the larger ones weighed more than a ton. What was to be done about them? First, they would have to be cut apart.

During my absence, my determined nephew had located some Korean artisans who were masters of the ancient art of stonecutting. First they began by locating what appeared to be a seam, or fissure, along which they drilled a series of holes with a diamond bit. Into each hole they inserted a broad, tough steel blade. Then, at the same moment, each struck his blade with a sledge hammer and the huge stone fell apart, as if bewitched. Success depended not only on their skill, but on their detailed knowledge of the stone's structure.

Already the bulk of the granite blocks, plus the smaller gravestones, were neatly stacked near the building location. They were lovely to behold; age and the weather had given them a deep, lustrous coloring.

Next, we tackled the excavating for the school itself. I decided to use manpower to do this job, for parts of the site were hilly and other parts swampy. It would have been far less expensive to use power diggers, but I wanted to give work to the laborers. They still could earn scarcely more than a dollar a day even though they worked from seven in the morning until seven in the evening, taking an hour for lunch, a half-

hour break at mid-morning, and another one in the middle of
the afternoon.

We got off to a good start. But we soon ran into rock. After
that, we met more rock and still more rock. The foreman came
to me and reported,

"We're going to have to use dynamite."

"So much the better," I replied. "Then we'll have some rock
to use for building the base of our road."

I couldn't help laughing when, a few days later, we discovered that on the back of our property we had a stone quarry!
We had no need to hoard our rocks. Here, right under our
noses, were all we could possibly use. I was reminded of something Albert Schweitzer once said: "I am rich in rocks."

But we could not look upon rock as such an asset when it
came to digging a well. There was water underneath, perhaps,
but over it was rock.

Like Moses, we struck the rock. But we used dynamite instead of a rod. And the water came gushing forth. We are
proud of our water in Korea. We like to think that it personi-
fies the spirit of our people—it is always clear and sparkling.

The next event in our building program was the laying of
the cornerstone. I selected July 4 for this ceremony because I
also consider this day of special significance: It is the day on
which a nation of men became politically free.

But we needed all the time in the intervening two months to
blast out enough rock to make a place for the cornerstone.

About this time, I discovered that although the building
itself was progressing, the funds for erecting it were diminish-
ing. Since I had undertaken the project, all construction items
had gone up in price by at least 2 or 3 per cent—timber, gravel,
cement, everything.

Wherever I turned, I could see no way out. I could only
pray to God for help.

The next few weeks were among the most exciting of my
life. Things happened one after another at such a speed that it

made my head swim. In faith and confidence I had given orders for the construction to proceed even though we did not have the money in hand.

By this time we had sold the buildings in Washington for about $35,000. With the money I had earned from my lectures, the sale of *September Monkey,* and various gifts, I could count on about $55,000. But since the building was going to cost around $85,000 to complete, I was still $30,000 short.

Then one morning in May, out of the blue, came a letter from America with the great good news. It was from Stanley Kresge. He wanted to let me know that the Kresge Foundation had agreed to contribute $15,000 to the Induk Vocational School *provided* I would be able to raise a matching amount.

You may be sure that I got busy. In the next week I wrote more than forty letters to friends all over the United States and Canada.

Within ten days, the returns began to come in to my office in Washington, which in my absence was being run by my daughter. She cabled me at once, so I could share her delight. Many, many other checks were sent as tokens of loyalty and support—some from Sunday School classes, some from individuals—five, ten, fifteen, twenty-five dollars in an envelope.

More than $3,000 was immediately in hand. At that point I totaled things up again.

I knew that all my friends had contributed to the limit of their abilities at the moment. The Berea in Korea Foundation had committed every cent it had available. There was no source anywhere in sight—and I was still almost $12,000 short of what I needed. I simply put the problem in God's hands.

I have always found that out of desperation comes inspiration. If you let it rest there—nothing happens. But if you add perspiration—then results are sure to follow.

The inspiration was not long in coming. When it did come, it was so clear and so convincing, I could only wonder why I had not thought of it before. But I could not tell how valid it was until I put it to the test.

I sat down with my No. 2 yellow pencil and counted up seven contractors who were supplying materials for the school: concrete, tile, electricity, plumbing, lumber, and so on. Then I went to call on them, one by one.

"Look here," I said to them, in effect. "The building of this school is being made possible by the generosity of our friends in the United States and Canada. But when the school is finished, it will be for the purpose of giving an education to our own village boys. Does your conscience allow you to make a profit on such an undertaking?"

Each man to whom I spoke admitted that although either he had not known about this aspect of the job, or had not thought about it, now that the facts had been presented to him he certainly did not want to profit by it.

"Then," I added quickly, "all I am asking is that you contribute your profit margin to me in the form of a voluntary gift."

No one refused me. I had taken them by surprise. But I think that they were pleased as well as proud to feel that they had a part in this exciting experiment.

Inside of another week I was able to instruct Iris to tell Mr. Kresge his specifications had been met. A few days later she cabled back that the check from the Foundation had arrived in Washington and had been duly deposited to the account of "Berea in Korea."

Indeed, those were happy days that followed. The cornerstone had been laid; the foundations had been completed; the granite slabs had been turned into steps and a walkway leading to the front door; the framework was rising.

Almost every day whenever I could spare the time I went out to the building site to relish the experience of seeing my dream take on substance and form right before my eyes. So many obstacles had been overcome—obstacles that had seemed insurmountable at the time they first appeared. From here on in, I would know nothing but the sheer joy of fulfillment. Or so I thought.

One day in mid-July, while I was immersed in this happy mood, my nephew phoned me and invited me to dine with him at our favorite rendezvous, Korea House.

We enjoyed a delightful meal. During the course of it we spoke only of family affairs, not mentioning a word of business. It did occur to me, however, that my nephew was not quite his usual enthusiastic self. Rather, he seemed somewhat quiet and subdued.

It was not until we had finished the last taste of the small, delicate pears which we Koreans like to have for dessert, that he got out his pencil and pad and laid them beside his plate. A frown creased his forehead.

"Auntie," he began slowly, "I haven't said anything to you about it, but I've been spending the last couple of weeks visiting with the various contractors and suppliers. You may have wondered why the heating system hasn't been installed."

I had to confess I hadn't given it much thought.

"You've probably read about all the new building that's going on in Korea—and on the whole I think we should be pleased."

I wondered why he was digressing from the subject like that. But I waited.

"The unfortunate side of it is that the demand is creating a shortage of materials of all kinds."

He paused.

"So naturally, the prices not only have gone up—they have risen fantastically."

By now I had a good idea of what he was going to say, but I was speechless.

He made a few doodles with his pencil, then laid it beside

the pad, folded his arms, and looked at me directly.

"Auntie, I guess there's no easy way to tell you. I have received the latest figures from all the builders. Even foregoing the profit, the school is now going to cost twenty-five thousand dollars more than we counted on."

"Twenty-five thousand dollars!"

The earth seemed to open beneath me. Once more I found myself in an impossible situation. I had already scraped the bottom of the barrel, so to speak. There was nowhere I could turn. But I couldn't quit. A Korean proverb came to my mind:

"Once you start dancing, so long as the music plays, you cannot stop."

Why had this happened to me? Was my life to be a treadmill from which I was never to be released? Or was I to be led so close to seeing my dream come true, only to have it denied when it was almost within my grasp?

No, I did not believe it. I would not believe it. In my heart I knew that God had other plans. I need only wait until He chose to show me what I ought to do.

At the moment, I was obsessed with one thought: Where in the world was I going to raise $25,000?

The shattering revelation of my nephew took place on a Friday evening. Since the next day was a Saturday, there wasn't much I could do right away. Besides, God had not yet seen fit to disclose what my plan should be.

At the time, I was staying at the home of a young woman friend named Chin Chai Kim. Chin Chai was about the same age as my daughter Iris.

We were very close, for during the Korean War Chin Chai had undergone an emotional experience very much like that endured by Iris. She, too, had lost her husband.

I was sitting on the second-story veranda the following day, enjoying my afternoon tea, when Chin Chai came home from a shopping spree downtown. The weather, I remember, was beautiful—mild, but not too warm.

I invited Chin Chai to join me in a cup, and she sat down. We visited a while, chatting idly of this and that. Perhaps I appeared rather abstracted, because presently she asked if anything was bothering me. In a few minutes, seeing that I had a sympathetic listener, I poured out the whole story. I told her about the building program, how I'd thought everything was solved, and then how I'd been caught in the squeeze of rapidly rising prices.

I often wondered afterward, how it was that Chin Chai, who was just the right person, happened to turn up at the right psychological moment?

Most people—especially my women friends—might have been inclined to cluck over me and sympathize with me. Not so Chin Chai. She'd had some business experience, and she thought logically, realistically, like a man. She listened to me with a faraway look in her eye which indicated that her mind was working. Now and then she would shoot a question at me, which was both shrewd and penetrating.

"But if prices are going up in one field, they must be going up in others as well," she observed.

"Yes, I expect that is so," I replied rather vaguely. If pressed, I would have to admit that I had not been paying much attention to anything going on in the world except the building of my school and the raising of money to pay my bills.

"Australian wool, for example," Chin Chai continued. "I hear Australian wool has been going up by leaps and bounds."

"Yes, I imagine it has," I said, nodding. Since it hadn't been necessary for me to buy Australian wool for the school, I really wasn't very much interested.

There was a slight click as Chin Chai put down her cup on

the saucer. She was staring out at Nam San Mountain in the distance and seemed lost in thought.

Then she said, almost as if to herself,

"If I understood you correctly, you did say that you had dollars in your accounts in America."

I replied that this was true. Oh, I had dollars all right. Dollars sitting on deposit back there in banks in the United States. But every dollar was committed; each one had its job cut out for it, or I wouldn't be in the fix I was in now.

"Too bad you're not a different kind of person," she said. "Too bad you haven't had more business experience."

"Why do you say that?" I asked.

"I was just thinking as you spoke," she went on, "that if you knew what you were doing and had the nerve to try, you could turn a pretty penny."

"How?"

"By becoming an international trader."

"What do you mean by that exactly?" I asked.

"By buying wool in Australia for dollars and selling it again in Korea for *won* [the Korean unit of exchange]. Of course, the deal wouldn't be any good unless you were going to spend your money in Korea."

I tried to control my excitement. God had showed me the way. The rest was up to me.

"How would you go about it?" I inquired calmly. "What would be the first step?"

"Well," Chin Chai answered, "if I were going to do it, I think I would first discuss the matter with our Minister of Finance. Then I'd go see the Minister of Commerce and Industry to make sure that the necessary papers were in order. Then I would—but why are you asking me all these questions?"

I was laughing so hard inside, it was all I could do to keep from laughing audibly. Go see the Minister of Finance! Have an interview with the Minister of Commerce and Industry! I, a woman? And one totally inexperienced in such matters of high finance?

We had made much progress in Korea in recent years, to be sure, but that sort of thing still wasn't done. For a woman even to ask for an interview with highly placed members of the government would be considered an impertinence. And to seek permission for such a ridiculous, hare-brained scheme was unthinkable. Why, they would show me out of their offices! Nevertheless, as we sipped our tea, I kept right on pressing Chin Chai for details, trying to squeeze every last bit of useful information out of her.

It was only after she had gone to take care of her domestic affairs that the full enormity of what I was contemplating came over me. I, Induk Pahk, lecturer, acting as an international trader? Or why not call it by its true name—gambler?

Yes, a gambler!

Moreover, I was preparing to gamble with the funds belonging to the Berea in Korea Foundation. If I did not win, it could mean disaster. I could lose at least $25,000, maybe more. I might very well lose everything. And then where would I be? Where would the school be? On the other hand, if I did not gamble, if I took no chances, I would be right where I was now—nowhere.

After all, when you come right down to it, why shouldn't I gamble?

Wasn't I a tiger?

I could do nothing until Monday. At least I had that much time to think out my plan of action or to withdraw if I lost my nerve. Instead of wasting my energies in a welter of indecision, looking at first this possibility and then that one, I decided I would spend the hours "getting in character" rehearsing for my new role.

This was going to be a difficult part for me as a woman to play, for I had never known any gamblers and very few international traders. How should I act in order to arouse the maximum business confidence in my new business associates? How should I dress? What manner should I assume in order to put my best foot forward? Ought I to smile? Should I look solemn?

Reluctantly, I reached the conclusion that it was all a lot of nonsense. I was not being myself; I was planning to be an impostor, something I had never done before. Just at that moment a most useful piece of wisdom came to me, something that my mother had told me long ago. It was, in fact, a piece of wisdom that promised to solve everything. At any rate, it enabled me to fall asleep that night. It was, very simply:

"Help them to help you!"

It was so obvious. Why hadn't I thought of it before? Here was the cardinal rule for anyone who finds himself in the position I was in. Most people would like to help. In fact, they are often eager to help. But they want, above all else, to be told how to do it. Instead, the conversation usually skitters all around the subject. Obscurities, digressions, and antagonisms arise; sometimes an interview is terminated without the objective ever having been touched on, in spite of the fact that it is usually what both parties desire most of all.

"Help them to help you!"

Once I had grasped that principle as my solution, then I could forget all about putting on any false airs or trying to assume an artificial personality. I was able to concentrate on being myself and on finding the most eloquent way of stating what was on my mind.

Monday morning came all too soon. Quite early, I presented myself according to plan at the office of the Minister of Commerce and Industry.

The interview went with surprising smoothness, because I had the confidence of abiding faith in God and was concentrating on one thought:

"I want to help him to help me."

The next interview went smoothly, and so did the next.

At the office of the Minister of Finance the situation took a new turn.

"Before I can issue a permit for the transaction," the Minister said, "your bank balance in the United States must be certified by the Korean Embassy in Washington, D.C."

I could foresee a long delay. The building program would remain at a standstill while my venture in high finance became hopelessly snarled in red tape. I should have anticipated that something like this would happen. After all, I was a woman. I wasn't supposed to know about such matters.

But I was determined that it was not going to happen to me.

Later in the afternoon, at the first opportune moment, I put in a long-distance telephone call to Iris who was back in Washington. I explained the situation to her in great detail. I think that was the longest long-distance call that I have ever made. I talked for one hour and forty minutes, and the bill was almost $400.

When I was about halfway through, Iris, whom I had trained to be frugal, suddenly cried out in horror,

"But Mother! I wonder if you realize you are talking long distance from Korea! This telephone call must be costing you a fortune!"

"Concentrate on what I'm telling you!" I snapped. Then with all the *savoir-faire* of the international gambler, I added, "You don't understand. I'm involved in a twenty-five-thousand-dollar deal!"

Time dragged by on leaden feet during the next week. Every day I watched the international commodities market, fearful lest Australian wool go into a long downward slide.

But—soon enough—eight days later, the certification from the Korean Embassy was in my hands, and the permit was soon forthcoming.

The time had come to act. It took all the courage at my command.

I must say I held my breath when I committed almost all the money the Foundation had at its disposal to the purchase of a large block of virgin wool from the firm of McGregor & Sons, Co., Ltd., in Melbourne, Australia, through their Tokyo office. And I must admit that I gave a great sigh of relief several days later when the wool was safely sold to the First Woolen Textile Company in Seoul.

I had made a nice profit on the transaction. In fact, the exact figure was $25,000—almost precisely what I needed.

In some ways, from the standpoint of strain, it was the hardest money I ever earned. I think if I had the choice, I would prefer to travel up and down the land, earning it by my lectures, a few dollars at a time.

11

*

Faith Moves a Mountain

ONCE THE FINANCIAL crisis had been solved, I made preparations to return immediately to the United States since I had some important plans to carry out. For almost a year I had been preparing for the dedication of the two school buildings to take place on my next birthday, September 24.

Literally hosts of my friends had taken part with me in making the school a reality. They had given unstintingly of their help—financially and spiritually. I wanted as many of them as possible to be with me at the dedication ceremonies. For that reason I had been corresponding with them all through the year.

Upon my return I found that sixteen of my friends, fourteen from the United States and two from Canada, were able to spare both the time and the money and would accompany me to Korea.

I planned a sight-seeing tour for my traveling companions en route, with stopovers in Honolulu, Manila, Bangkok, Singapore, Hong Kong, Taiwan, and Japan. We were a happy and congenial group and greatly enjoyed all our experiences in the course of our travels.

This trip not only filled me with personal enthusiasm, but made me glow with natural pride. To the best of my knowledge, this was the first time that a large party of tourists had headed west with Korea as the target destination, rather than as a stop along the way to some other point in the Orient.

Thirty days after leaving San Francisco, we landed at Kimpo Airport on September 23, the day before the dedication ceremonies were to be held. The plane touched down shortly after 1:00 P.M. I barely had time to get to the hotel, change my clothes, and get out to the school that same afternoon.

It had been almost two months since I had been able to check up on progress, and I wasn't sure what I would find. The buildings were not quite finished, but then I hadn't expected them to be and had prepared my guests for the situation. Aside from that, everything was in good order and all going to my satisfaction.

The day of the dedication dawned bright and clear. The ceremonies were held both outside the entrance, on the unfinished terrace, and inside, in the "lobby to be."

The approach to the school which had been no more than a scar in the earth when I saw it last was now a finished road. It was banked on both sides with masses of cosmos, my favorite flower, in lovely pastel shades of pink and lavender.

Over the doorway someone had lettered on a white cloth in black letters a huge sign, "WELCOME!" Underneath it was the Korean equivalent in Hangul, "WHAN YOUNG!"

The ceremony, conducted by the Rev. Young Bin Im, General Secretary of the Korean Bible Society, went off beautifully. Of the many significant statements, one in particular has remained in mind ever since, because it has such universal application. It was made by Merwyn Skidmore, a retired business executive and husband of one of my friends. He said,

"Wherever we go we leave part of ourselves behind and take a part of others with us. I leave a part of myself here and take something of you with me."

That night about thirty of my friends gave me a surprise birthday party at Korea House. The main dishes were Korean, but the dessert was American, a huge cake on which was written "Happy Birthday" in flowing script. In deference to my American and Canadian friends, we sat in chairs around tables, instead of cross-legged on the floor, as is usually the custom in Korean restaurants.

The following morning I took my group to the top of Nam San (South Mountain). I wanted my friends to have a good view of the city of Seoul which lay spread out below. I tried to describe to them the beauty and picturesqueness of the old city from which the Yi Dynasty ruled the country for more than five centuries. Then I explained that the city below them was all new. The old city had been leveled by the Communist bombings during the Korean War. Fortunately, a few historic landmarks such as the old palace had been spared. But most of the official structures were gone.

The city today, I told them, was a mingling of the old and the new. The new city had many advantages such as broad, tree-lined boulevards and fine, modern buildings. But much of the flavor of the old city had been lost.

While we looked out at the beautiful view, I gave my friends some facts about my country. Korea, a peninsula, is about the size of the state of Minnesota and is situated in a most strategic spot in the Far East. It is a land bridge, a transition zone, and a buffer state between Japan and Russia, Japan and China. In the days when China was all-powerful, Korea was kept as a protectorate by that nation. But when China became weak, the young and ambitious Japan took over Korea by beating China in 1894, then beating Russia in 1904. It was a great blow to Russia to be blocked by Japan and not to be able to get her hands on Korea; for Russia had no ice-free ports on the Pacific and wanted to have access to that ocean through Korea. (Russia borders on Korea for twelve miles.)

In 1945, after Japan's defeat in World War II, Korea, under trusteeship of the U.N. pending independence, was divided into provisional occupation zones at the 38th parallel, the Russian Army occupying the north, the U.S. forces the south. In 1950, the Russians defied U.N. recognition of South Korea as the recognized government of the entire nation. A North Korean Army crossed the parallel and the war began.

Into South Korea streamed five million refugees from the North—with empty hands. The South also was deprived of the rich mineral deposits, timber, water power, and industries of the North—all of which fell into the hands of the Communists. In the South we have rich farm lands, and also some water power, but little in the way of minerals. We have twenty-five million people living in 37,425 square miles—giving a population density of 668 per square mile. Therefore, South Korea has the third highest population density in Asia, after Formosa and Japan. North Korea, has only 210 inhabitants per square mile, and 10,436 square miles *more* than South Korea.

As one of South Korea's thinking persons I ask myself what must I do to help my country—with poverty so rampant. We Koreans are thankful for the aid extended to us by the United States and other countries, but we feel we cannot rely upon such a crutch for long. We must eventually become self-reliant. Furthermore, we might as well face the fact that we are destined to live in the same location—opposite Red China with its seven hundred million as well as the U.S.S.R. and Japan. And so we are concerned with what would be the best formula to save ourselves and to win over our neighbors. Not by hate, certainly—rather by love.

The Communists deprived us of many of our natural resources. But they could not take from us the one irreplaceable resource, hope.

It is hope that has enabled us to survive.

A few days later I saw my friends off on the plane for America. I stayed for about a month to oversee my wool transactions, then I, too, returned to the United States to resume my lecturing.

I had just returned from Florida that winter of 1963-64. I was in a high state of anticipation because my school was about to be opened and I was preparing to go back to Korea.

When only a few days remained before my departure, Iris asked me to have dinner with her and a friend of hers in observance of the Chinese New Year at the Peking Restaurant in Washington. I thought this was a nice gesture and accepted with pleasure.

I was taken completely by surprise, as we entered the upstairs dining room, for thirty-five people stood up to greet us. They had been asked to come to a send-off party given us by my lawyer, Mr. Carliner, and his wife.

The Carliners had contrived to invite people not only from the Washington area but from far away without my ever finding out about it.

Among them were my old friends Ethel Dean and Doris Courtice who had opened up Canada for me. I had first come to know them at the Camp Farthest Out retreat at Whitby, Ontario. They had invited me to speak the following year before their Ladies' Bible class at St. David's United Church in Toronto. I have repeated my appearance before that class every year since. Today I feel that I am part of Canada and

Canada is part of me, just as I feel I am part of the United States.

A few days later I was gliding through the air, Korea-bound, on the journey that had by now become so familiar to me.

There was much to do, and not much time in which to do it. In Korea, the school year begins in March. (We have shorter summer vacations and longer winter ones in order to conserve fuel.) We had yet to choose the thirty boys who would be admitted for the first semester. Also, we hoped to have everything in shape for the opening. It was now February, and I could not tell from the reports I had been receiving how far along preparations were. However, I would soon be on the spot and would be able to see for myself.

As I got out of the taxi with my nephew on that cold, raw February afternoon and climbed the frozen road up the hill, one thought went through my mind:

"It's all so new! New! New! New! Here is something altogether new in this old land!"

I think that was the thrill of it. This was the zero hour. The future history of the school lay ahead of me, a blank piece of paper on which it was up to me to write.

Even the road on which I was walking was new. No vehicle had ever passed over it except those containing the construction materials.

In my imagination, I could hear the energetic step of future schoolboys who would pass this way. I could hear their laughter, the echo of their shouts, the sounds of life!

I looked up the hill and there it was—the school itself! The architect had done himself proud. The green of the slate roof, just above the walls, with their alternate panels of white stucco and red brick framing the large picture windows, gave a feeling of harmony.

The sight filled me with exhilaration. It had happened, un-

believably, since I had seen it last. And it was everything that
I had hoped it would be.

But then my eye went first to the right and then to the left.
Everywhere was chaos. On all sides, brown frozen earth,
scarred with activity. And everywhere, leftover materials:
bricks, timber, concrete blocks, pipes, sacks of cement.

I tried to put myself in the position of a new boy coming to
school. How would this confusion appear to me under such
circumstances? I did not think that I would like it. As a matter
of fact, Kun Kong, the dormitory master who was sensitive to
this situation, said to the boys some time later:

"Don't forget, boys, these things didn't walk here by themselves. They were brought for a purpose. When their purpose
has been served they will disappear. And remember, too, they
may not look pretty lying around like this, but they cost a great
deal of money!"

To soothe myself, I sought the view of the distant mountains. But I could not find it. Then I discovered it was blocked
by a high hill right on the southeast corner of the property. The
very sight of that hill infuriated me. I wondered why I hadn't
noticed before how obstructive it was. I suppose because prior
to the time the building went up I had thought of the location
all as wild land. It hadn't mattered so much before whether the
land had contained a high hill or swampy valley. I turned to
my nephew.

"You see that hill over there? That hill must go."

"But, Auntie!" he gasped. "Do you know what's involved in
that? It would take fifty men working, oh. . . ." He ticked off
some figures to himself for a moment. "Yes, fifty men working
ten hours a day, seven days a week"—he paused dramatically
—"four months, Auntie; it would take them four months to
level it. And when you are through, the mountain of your debt
will be higher than the hill you removed. And I know how you
hate debts," he finished, slightly out of breath.

"Oho!" I pounced on him. "Then you have been thinking along the same lines I have—that the hill is a distraction—or you would not have been able to reel off all those calculations."

"Yes," he admitted, "I did give it some thought, but I was forced to dismiss removing it as impractical."

"All right, then," I said, "we'll get a bulldozer."

"A bulldozer!"

He looked at me as though that was the kind of suggestion one would naturally expect from a woman.

But at least he did not immediately denounce it.

Feeling a trifle triumphant, I went from the chaos of the yard into the school itself, hoping to satisfy my sense of order.

When I entered the building, I had still another shock. It was beautiful on the outside. But within, nothing was finished. The floors were made of terrazzo stone, decorated with a beautiful Korean design executed by my nephew. But the floors were not polished. One corridor did not even have any design in it yet.

"Nephew," I said, "in a few weeks our students are coming. This building must be ready for them."

Again he gasped.

"But Auntie! With one machine, it will take months just to polish the floors."

"Then get many machines! Get every machine in Seoul!"

I said it, even though I didn't think it was possible. I was whistling in the dark.

We went on to inspect the large soccer field which had been placed in front of the school building down the hill. There were no steps leading to it.

By this time my viewpoint had changed. Where, a few minutes ago, I had thought of everything as fresh and new, now I

thought of it as raw—just raw! Raw weather outside, everything raw inside. Raw earth, raw floors—they seemed all a
part of the same rawness.

I was on the point of despair. Nothing was the way I had
hoped it would be.

I had deluded myself with my romantic ideas. I could not
think of letting our first class of village boys, arriving with
such high hopes and expectations, derive their first impressions
of what the school was going to be like from such a chaotic
mess!

I was feeling somewhat downcast as my nephew and I set
out on a tour of inspection. We went in to have a look at the
washroom. Absent-mindedly I turned a faucet. Water gushed
forth! Hardly daring to believe it, I put my fingers on the
radiator and drew them away hastily. We had heat! I pressed a
button and a light came on. We had electricity!

We went on into the dormitories. The bunk beds were standing neatly in the rooms, ready to receive the occupants.

My viewpoint underwent a rapid change again. Why, the
boys had all the essentials of life! They would be warm, comfortable, and clean. It might be good for them to do a little
pioneering in the beginning and to be there to watch the chaos
cleared away.

"Good heavens!" I thought to myself. "What am I worried
about?"

With our school soon scheduled to open, we had placed
announcements in the three leading newspapers of Seoul. We
wanted especially to reach underprivileged boys, boys who
would have no other opportunity for education, many of
whom would be living in remote places. But in Korea the
papers of Seoul are also national. Word travels rapidly, penetrating into far-off nooks and crannies. We had no doubt that

these announcements would get to the boys we wanted to reach.

But we were not prepared for the avalanche of application letters that came to us in response.

Every day brought more. They piled up on my desk in the administration office. I was pleased at first by the size of the response and therefore not immediately aware of the heartbreak that was to follow.

The school did offer an attractive prospect to poor boys hungry for an education. We had agreed that we would charge a tuition fee of two dollars per month. But room and board would be free. I had learned from my study of the administration of orphanages that it was unwise to give everything absolutely free. Once the children became accustomed to this situation, they came to expect it and found it all the harder to make the adjustment to the realities of working for a living.

All the boys would be required to work two hours a day, either in keeping up the school or in running the farm, as a contribution toward their board and room. This was in accord with the original Berea idea.

From a financial standpoint, what they could earn on the school farm would not defray as much as one seventh of the cost. But from the psychological standpoint it was all important, for it satisfied their feeling of pride and independence.

I know that it may be hard for my Western readers to comprehend, but some of the boys' families were so poor that they found it a hardship to raise even so small a sum as two dollars. The school helped in whatever ways it could, sometimes deferring payment when necessary. Somehow, even though it meant denying themselves the necessities of life to do so, the families managed to meet the payments.

By the time the day came for the entrance examinations, we had one hundred and forty applicants. And we had room for no more than thirty boys.

We had worked out some kind of examination with questions, both oral and written, which we hoped would be of help to us in the weeding-out process. But remember, everything was experimental. We were feeling our way; nothing was fixed.

Mr. T. S. Lee, our teacher in charge of agriculture, took care of the farming side, and Mr. Kong, our chaplain and dormitory supervisor, also taught such subjects as history, geography, and Korean literature. My nephew, who was administrator of the school, taught economics and business administration. Mr. H. K. Park had mathematics and lab subjects, such as physics and chemistry. Larry Lewis, a GI, taught English conversation, and Mr. K. J. Park taught English reading and grammar.

The day came when the one hundred and forty boys gathered in the classrooms to answer the questions on the entrance examinations. They all wore the uniforms of their junior high schools. Many came with no coats, even though the February weather was biting cold.

The shuffle of feet and rustle of papers were the only sounds to be heard as they set about their tasks. Only the intense look in their eyes and the determined lines of their jaws betrayed the fierceness of the competition. This was obvious, too, in the all-out effort they put into trying to beat each other when it came to running the 100-meter dash, which was part of the physical fitness test.

The exams helped. But we could not be guided by them entirely. It was all too new. We had to keep our decisions flexible enough to allow for human situations.

When they came to the question at the end of the examination, "Are you interested in farming?" nearly all of them answered "Yes." Naturally, because that's what they were here for.

One boy, however, put down as his answer,

"I can't say that farming really interests me. But I am curious about it."

I thought that this forthright, honest, and original statement indicated such a strong and unusual character that I included his name among those boys who were to be admitted.

We informed the boys that in four days the names of those who had been accepted would be posted on a large signboard on the outside of the building.

The difficult job of choosing the boys was finished. I felt not only relieved but uplifted as I set out for the railroad station to take the train to Seoul. Suddenly it occurred to me that we had no school song, and the boys would be coming soon. I thought, "What is the theme of the school; what is our chief work?" I was reminded of a poem by John Greenleaf Whittier:

> I hear the tread of pioneers
> of nations yet to be;
> The first low wash of waves, where soon
> shall roll a human sea.
>
> The rudiments of empire here
> Are plastic yet and warm;
> The chaos of a mighty world
> Is rounding into form!
>
> Each rude and jostling fragment soon
> Its fitting place shall find,—
> The raw material of a state,
> Its muscle and its mind!

"Why, we will be forging character, forging manhood," I said to myself. "Then why not the tune to Verdi's lovely 'Anvil Chorus'?"

On that beautiful spring afternoon, as I made my way down the hill to the station, my steps started beating out the music.

It was the tune I wanted! I knew it was the tune. I started

humming. After all, you had to have a tune before you could have a song.

As I continued humming, the words came tumbling into my head. I should say that in two or three minutes I had the song all written—long before I reached the station.

Kyo Kah [School Song]
Behind the Sam Kok San [Three Horned Mountain],
Before the flowing Joong Nang Chun [stream],
Stands Induk Vocational School.
Pride and treasure of our nation,
Blessed by God,
And chosen are we.
Let us march with vigor to our work
With implements in hand,
A thought in mind to discover and create.
Glorious forever.

At the first opportunity I tried the song out on Mr. Kong. He pursed his lips, looking skeptical.

"It's a little hard to sing," he said doubtfully. "Especially in the part where the melody goes up the scale so fast. But it has spirit, that's the main thing. Yes, it does have spirit."

It was another raw, gray, chilly day in February. From quite early in the morning, I watched the boys coming up the hill: running, leaping, bouncing, jostling one another in their anxiety to see whether their names were on the board.

I saw them go running up and begin to scan the lists, their eyes bright, full of hope. Slowly the light would fade from some of their faces, their shoulders slumped with defeat. Slowly, slowly these boys turned, to plod their way down the hill which they had run up so eagerly moments before.

Some looked as though they had just heard a sentence of death pronounced on them—and, indeed, they had. The fact that they had not been accepted meant that the last chance for an education, the last chance to improve their lot, had passed them by. For where was the money to come from for their schooling? Nowhere—aside from here. It was as simple and as tragic as that.

Then—in contrast—here and there in the crowd were boys who, having seen their names on the board, jumped up and down like awkward puppets, unable to contain the joy of being accepted.

Tears blurred my vision. I needed the presence of my mother to stand at my elbow and say, "Don't cry. If it makes you cry, you shouldn't have done it."

Anger overcame me. I wanted to strike out blindly. Why did things have to be like this? Why did these boys have to be denied their life's opportunity, when so little would make the difference!

And especially when others had so much—more than they knew what to do with.

I asked the question that millions had asked before me, and millions more would still be asking after I was gone, "Why? Why?"

I remembered seeing President Kennedy on television once when he said sorrowfully, "Life is unfair."

Those words remained with me, for to me they typified his insight and his compassion.

All right; so life is unfair. But we didn't have to take it lying down. We could try to do something about it.

I knew then, more fully than ever before, why I traveled and lectured constantly, why I kept going like a mad woman: It was all to change the look on the face of just one Korean boy.

Then the comment of a wise friend came to me:

"Never forget—the Red Sea didn't part until at least one Israelite waded in."

I was determined to do something. The voice of the Dragon spoke to quiet the Tiger,

"Be calm, go slow, take it easy. Don't forget—you have no more money. And you know how you hate to be in debt."

I went back to my desk and sat there thinking. If I could change the expression on the face of just one boy! I recalled our tour of inspection. I remembered a dormitory wing—it was unfinished; it had no bunks; we had not equipped it because we had agreed that we could feed and house no more than thirty boys.

A light dawned on me.

Why thirty? Why limit the number arbitrarily? Why not face the fact that it only reflected the limit I was setting on my own capacities?

I sent for my nephew.

"Nephew," I said, "when school opens next year, Induk Vocational School will admit thirty more boys, making sixty in all."

Before he could recover his breath and begin to argue with me, I added,

"And two years from that time we will make room for ninety boys."

When he pulled himself together, his sentiments were almost identical with the counsel of the Dragon.

"You have the wing waiting," I reminded him. "Your only cost will be to put in the bunk beds."

He laughed drily.

"You are forgetting, Auntie, that boys eat. And if I may remind you, they have the appetites of oxen. Also, I would like to call to your attention"—what little composure he had left now fled completely—"Auntie, you have no money—none."

I bristled.

"Then I will raise the money. What's the matter? Don't you have any faith in me?"

I had him there. Since I was his elder, he could hardly admit that this was so. It would have been too disrespectful.

Brave words! Now it was up to me to match them with bold deeds. But this was not going to be so easy. I was far from North America and the lecture circuit and the places where I could sell *September Monkey*. My friends had been giving and giving and giving. I could not expect them to respond to my cries of "Emergency!" indefinitely.

I would have to solve this dilemma on my own. God had not yet disclosed to me the course that I should take. But I was not concerned. I had every confidence that He would do so, all in His own good time.

Then, an important development began to take shape, one that I hadn't counted on. It had never occurred to me that a dream, once it becomes real, has hands and feet and makes demands on your time twenty-four hours a day, like a baby.

For thirty-five years I had carried my dream school in my head. It was very convenient there. I could visit it whenever I liked and think kindly and gratifying thoughts about it. I could speak of it enthusiastically without ever having to prove anything, except, when the spirit moved me, to show pictures of the site where someday the school would exist.

Now, from the moment it came into being, I was finding that a school seemed nothing but a collection of inconveniences. Take the payroll, for example. Who would ever have pictured "September Monkey" with a payroll to meet—and a payroll of twelve people, each one with at least five people dependent on him for support. In other words, in the twinkling of an eye, "September Monkey" had some sixty mouths to feed. That's where her dreaming about a school had gotten her!

It was a great day when the youngsters came swarming up the hill to start school. Each carried two *podaris*—one big one containing his bedding and one small one with his personal effects.

And if there were thirty boys, there must have been at least sixty people. Some boys, the refugees, or the sons of families who were too poor to afford bus fares, came alone. But many of the youngsters had been brought by members of their families.

Then something struck me that touched my heart and left me with a deepened sense of responsiblity.

Almost all of the relatives were women: mothers, grandmothers, sisters, in twos and threes, and even female cousins. What did this mean? That these were families torn apart. The fathers, the uncles, the older brothers were gone, all gone, lost in the war. Each boy was the precious one who remained—the breadwinner—on whom the others depended for their very existence. And they had entrusted that breadwinner to my care.

I felt very humble. Silently I addressed those shadows whose lives had been snuffed out in the tragedy.

"Thank you, Sirs," I said, "for sending us your sons. We will do our best for them and hope that they will one day lead better lives because of your sacrifice."

Now I was doubly glad I had ordered those thirty bunks.

12

*

To Change a Look

FOR THE FIRST hour or so of the opening day Induk Vocational School was in a state of happy pandemonium. Many of these boys had never before been outside their country villages, except for their trip to take the examination.

At one stroke, a whole new world was open to them. Everything we took for granted was fresh and new to them. For the moment we saw everything through their eyes and shared their wonder at it all.

They looked in amazement at the bunk beds when they were shown the places where they were going to sleep. Upon discovering the spring mattresses, they bounced up and down on them with endless cries of delight. (It is the Korean custom to sleep on quilts spread on the floor, whether one is rich or poor.) They ran wild in the bathrooms, turning the water on and off in the basins and showers, and flushing the toilets continuously. They never tired of pushing the buttons to make the electric lights go on and off, for in the villages from which they came they had known no light other than that from candles and kerosene lamps.

The boys soon settled into the routine. Mr. Kong, as dormitory supervisor, had done a wonderful job of having everything ready for them. In each room were two tiers of bunks and four cabinets for each boy to keep his clothes in, with shelves on top for books. Each room also had a table and four chairs, two on each side. Even the tables and chairs were new and strong.

All the smaller boys, who were usually quick and agile, were put in the top bunks, and the larger boys, who, on the whole, didn't move as quickly, went into the bunks below.

We had no disciplinary problem and no trouble getting the boys to study. They knew that if they failed they could not stay in school; they also knew that plenty of others were waiting to take their places.

So far as religion was concerned, many different points of view were represented among them. A number were of various Christian denominations: some Methodist, some Presbyterian, one Catholic, one Mormon. A few were Confucian, a few Buddhist; some had no religious belief whatever. Of these, quite a number embraced Christianity while they were at school, which was a source of great satisfaction to us.

Their day starts with a wake-up bell at 6:00 A.M. They have one-hour of clean-up time to get their rooms and corridors in order. Then follows ten minutes of some trepidation while Mr. Kong makes his tour of inspection. He insists that everything be as neat and spotless as a military school. It is the only way it can be.

The breakfast bell rings at 7:15. The boys start the routine with a different observance each day. On one occasion someone asks the blessing; another time, all sing a hymn; still another time, a boy may simply recite the motto on the wall of the school, "God first, others second, myself last."

This motto, incidentally, has had great meaning for me ever since I first encountered it. I never see it or hear it, but what I remember that day when I, a young woman new in the United

States, a little bit frightened, a little bit strange, was attending my first chapel at Wesleyan College in Macon, Georgia, where I was to go to school.

And I heard Dr. William F. Quillian, who was at that time the president say, " 'God first, others second, myself last.' That's what this school was founded for—to train all you young ladies to do likewise."

I always had it in mind to use this as my motto when "Berea in Korea" came into being. And with the continuation of my good fortune, I also had on the staff Mr. Kong, the man of many talents, who was able to render it for us in English in beautiful lettering.

After breakfast, before the nine o'clock class, we have chapel three times a week and outdoor exercises twice a week. We do not preach at chapel, but we try to help the boys feel that God is love and to expose them to uplifting thoughts.

Classes run until three. From three until five the boys work in the fields. From five to six they are free. After dinner the period until curfew at ten is devoted to homework.

We have to have penalties, of course. By trial and error, we soon found out what works best. If a boy makes the same mistake three times, he is asked to stay away from school for several days.

That is the worst punishment that he can experience because he wants above all to learn, since he values highly his opportunity to get an education.

One of the most important results our school could accomplish, I had long since decided, was to give training and experience in democracy. This was obviously necessary if the boys were to take part in co-ops or other farmers' organizations where working with others is an important consideration.

But beyond that, the very future of my country depended upon their effectiveness as citizens in acting independently.

Neither grandparents nor parents had much experience in thinking for themselves, having lived so long under the domination of the Japanese. Furthermore, Korean tradition put heavy stress on unquestioning obedience to elders. For these reasons, we had to start practically from the beginning.

The boys were given their first lesson in democracy when they were asked to choose a president and vice-president. Five months were allowed to go by before the election was held so they would get to know one another. Election day drew near, and three boys were picked to run for office; but when the time came, none wanted to be a candidate. Each boy was so shy and so lacking in self-confidence that he didn't want to make the required speech on his own behalf. One stood up and said, "I'm not worthy to be president. Why don't you cast your votes instead for one who is?" In spite of these diffident first steps, by the end of the year, the students were governing themselves through the medium of a student council and a student leader. All duties, such as ringing bells, cleaning the dormitories and classrooms, and even washing the dishes, were democratically parceled out.

Many of the boys had never washed a dish before; this duty had always been performed by their mothers or sisters. The boys did not complain, although a few of the parents did—but not for long. We liked to think that they were a help to their sisters after they got home, and that they treated them with a little more consideration.

In making their adjustment, the boys were helped tremendously by Mr. Kong, who had learned at firsthand through peril to his life, the value of democratic freedom. Mr. Kong was a refugee from the Communists in North Korea. I first met him at the Young Nok Presbyterian Church, where he was Sunday School superintendent. Young Nok, the largest Presbyterian church in Seoul, was built by the refugees from North

Korea. We had many conversations, and I was so impressed I invited him to become chaplain and senior teacher at our school.

Perhaps I would never have known the moving story of Mr. Kong's life if I had not noticed one day, soon after he joined us, that two of the fingers of his right hand were permanently bent and that he had a deep groove along the right side of his head.

It seems that Mr. Kong had been arrested in one of the revolts against Communist authority that had occurred with some frequency in North Korea. Along with many others, he had been taken out into a field and beaten over the head with cudgels wielded by Red soldiers.

Instinctively, he threw up his hand to ward off the blows. As result, his fingers became paralyzed, but the reflex action protected him and no doubt did much to save his life.

For eight hours he remained in an unconscious state, lying there surrounded by the dead and dying. When night fell, he was able to escape and finally made his way in safety from North Korea across the 38th Parallel to the South. But he was forced to leave behind him his beloved wife and two small sons.

When he thought back over what had happened, he concluded that since his life had been spared against such great odds, there must be some special purpose behind this miracle. Out of gratitude, he decided to devote his energies to the service of God.

In South Korea he worked his way through a college. Soon after graduation he began his activities for the church.

To be chaplain at our school fitted in with his concept of his life's calling. He lives in the dormitory with the students and supervises their activities.

The boys are his family now. In spite of constant inquiries, he has never learned anything as to the fate of his wife and children.

I had been so busy gloating over the way things were going inside the school that I had entirely neglected to deal with the debris outside.

But now it clamored for attention; I could ignore it no longer. The graves had been moved, to be sure, but the heavy slabs were scattered everywhere. Spring was coming and the earth was turning green, with the exception of our school grounds where everything was still brown and raw.

It was already getting late to begin the landscaping, for the rainy season which could play havoc with unprotected soil was almost upon us.

I was not long in learning, however, that landscaping is an expensive business. My investigations soon brought me face to face with the realization that our state of chaos was not merely physical—it was also financial, which was far more difficult to cope with.

The time had come, not only to face unpleasant facts, but to weigh them carefully. I tried smiling them away—but they did not smile back. Here were some of them:

Fact No. 1: I had blithely paid the first month's salaries for the school staff of twelve out of the Foundation's principal. But I could not possibly keep this up for very long.

Fact No. 2: To terrace the school grounds effectively against water erosion would take many, many pieces of sod, and sod was quite costly.

Fact No. 3: Mr. Lee, our agricultural leader, had just bought, at a very good price, five hundred chestnut trees and was making plans to buy three thousand more.

Now these trees would, in time, constitute a most valuable asset for the school, since Korean chestnuts are especially delicious and much in demand. But it would require a considerable outlay of cash, and this at a time when my mood was to pinch every penny until it cried. Also there were the forty-five gingko trees to line the approach to the school.

Fact No. 4: I was finding that you cannot start to farm simply by looking at the earth and commanding, "Grow!"

Seeds for rice, corn, red beans and soy beans, not to mention fertilizer and soil enrichers, cost a great deal of money.

Fact No. 5: I wanted to stock the farm with animals, and animals cost money.

"Agri-business" always appealed to me as a very fine phrase. But evidently I was not a very good agri-business-woman, because this expense came to me as a great surprise—and an unwelcome one to say the least!

Fact No. 6: We had as yet no athletic field for basketball and volleyball. It would be necessary to have one but this also was going to cost us quite a bit of money.

Fact No. 7: I was going to move that hill!

But the biggest fact on the list was the one that stated in no uncertain terms, "Sod this land before it washes away." Sodding has a different meaning for us than it does in the West, where, I believe, it is used to describe covering a surface with already rooted grass.

With us, the sod squares are used to provide terracing against erosion. This job was going to require at least ten thousand pieces of sod that would have to be taken up, transported, and put in position, to form a kind of gently sloping wall.

And all this had to be done quickly, before the spring rains could eat away the good topsoil.

But where was I going to get the money for such an undertaking, besides facing financially those six other nasty facts?

It so happened that at that time I had some unfinished business with McGregor & Sons, Co. Ltd. on my deal in Australian wool.

Since I had to go to their office every day anyway, I

thought, why not transact another deal in international trade?

I plunged again, but this time the situation was not so favorable. The exchange had shifted. I was, however, able to make a modest profit—enough to meet the payroll, pay for our orchard and chestnut trees, and plan an avenue that would be lined solidly with gingkoes.

So all that spring, I was not only starting a farm (without really knowing anything about it), I was also putting to the test some new educational theories of mine, and at the same time I was functioning as a big operator in international trade.

But alas! As soon as I managed to show a profit in one department, along came a crisis in another department which consumed it all. I could only hope that the farm and I would both keep our heads above water.

There's only one thing certain about the rainy season in Korea—you never can tell about it. Some years the sky manages only to squeeze out a few drops. In other years, the skies open up and the rain comes down in never-ending torrents.

In this crucial year we did very nicely up until July. Then the elements made up for lost time.

And why not? As I have said, I was born under the sign of the Dragon. And water is the Dragon's natural element. Everything was a struggle. The sod which we put in place one day was washed away the next. I could not see that we were making any progress. We took two steps forward and one step back. Meanwhile, our costs climbed upward.

To complicate matters further, I started to bring new animals to the school farm. And these cost money. Why was I so intent on doing this? All through the history of Korea, the heavy work has been done by the faithful ox, and next to him, the Korean man with his A-frame.

In the United States there is a saying, "Use your head and save your heels." It may be our weakness that we have never done this. All through our glorious past when we were producing scholars, poets, and artists, our country districts were blighted by grinding poverty. The possibilities for the learned man could be wonderful; but life held no future for the farmer, other than going to the rice fields with his ox. Now the time had come to make the transition from the ox to the tractor. Anyone can see that the latter is more economical. The tractor eats only when it works. But if the faithful ox is to go, then we have to stimulate the interest of the farmer in other animals.

I decided that we would stock our school farm with pigs, goats, chickens, and rabbits. About the time we were getting a start on our animal husbandry program, we heard a true story which stirred our imaginations.

A Korean farmer, well along in life, found himself in desperate straits after a long series of mishaps. He had his little plot of land and a very small sum of money.

He went to the American-Korean Foundation and said,

"I do not want charity. I have to my name five hundred *won* [about two dollars at that time]. But it is all that remains between me and destitution. Please advise me the best way to invest my capital so that I can keep from starving to death."

The Foundation gave him a loan in the form of a pair of pigs. Knowing that his very life depended on it, he treated those pigs like human beings. He studied their personalities, their psychology, their living habits. In time his affectionately meticulous care was rewarded. The farmer was presented with the fantastically large litter of fourteen piglets!

He gave the young pigs the same conscientious attention he had given their parents. All of them lived. Some he sold for their meat and some he kept for breeding. He began to get a reputation for the quality of his pork which soon commanded high prices. In the course of a few years, from this modest start he had become a solvent and successful pig farmer.

The boys loved to hear this story. We tried to put into practice the principles of studying the behavior patterns of animals as though they were persons. It is our plan to have a "piggy bank" through which we can loan little pigs to the graduates of our school in order to help them get a start in farming on their own.

Our location will prove to be a great asset, I am sure, when our school farm becomes a paying proposition. No more than five or six miles away, within easy reach by truck, the great city of Seoul, with its three and a half million population to be fed every day, offers a ready market for all we can raise.

Then, in the very midst of it everything, I was seized by an idea. I sent out an announcement stating that a public celebration of the opening of the school would be held on September 9.

All my friends thought that I must have gone out of my mind. As I looked around me, I must say I didn't much blame them.

The rain was still plummeting down. The landscaping was little more than half done. The granite blocks from the graveyard were lying all over the place like big white dominoes; the steps leading down to the soccer field before the main school building were not finished; the approach had no terraces; we still lacked a playing field for basketball and volleyball; I had taken no step toward moving the big hill; and the date of the celebration was only six weeks away. However, I let the announcement go out and now I was committed.

I had chosen that date deliberately. It could not be changed. There could be no other. September 9 marked the anniversary of that glorious day in 1945 when the American forces under General Hodge marched into Seoul to guarantee the independence of Korea. I would simply have to take my chances with the weather.

The rain continued, but we went on with the work in spite of it. I kept out of debt by additional deals in wool. All in all, these transactions must have brought me a profit of another $25,000.

The granite blocks from the graves found their way into

terraces, steps, flooring, and finally into a most unusual ornamental gate. Then, only a few days before the ceremony was to be held, we finished moving the high hill (using the dirt to fill in the swampy valley); we were now afforded a perfect view of the mountain and set about leveling off the site for a basketball and volleyball court.

For five successive days before the celebration, it rained—in fact, it did not merely rain, the heavens opened up and it seemed that God's oceans had overflowed. On the morning of the 9th, however—blue skies. As I scurried around making last-minute preparations, I looked at those skies and sent up ragged, breathless little prayers of thanksgiving.

More than three hundred guests arrived between 12:00 and 2:30. Many came by car and I was delighted to discover that the small playing field, where the hill used to be, made an excellent parking lot. Others came by train from Seoul, toiling up our hill on foot and exclaiming with awe, as they climbed. They strolled in twenty different directions—looking, admiring.

I wandered about, benumbed by nervous excitement, saying "Thank you" to all and sundry. An old Korean friend caught up with me and asked, "How are you?"

My response was a smile and an automatic, "Thank you, thank you!"

His polite expression dissolved into a grin as I gathered my wits about me. We chatted and I asked him how he had arrived.

"Why, by my No. 11 car," he responded.

I stared at him uncomprehendingly.

"You've been away too long, Induk," he chided. "Some fortunate Koreans have automobiles, but all Koreans have No. 11 cars!" And with that, he patted his legs.

Yes, I thought, I have been away too long—and yet, it was more than necessary; it was worthwhile.

The ceremonies were held in the dining room under three

flags, the flag of Korea in the center flanked by the flags of the United States and Canada, for it was my friends in these countries who had made my dream come true.

The principal speaker, the Director of Education for Seoul, had once been the teacher of my dear daughter Lotus. I paid tribute to all those who had helped.

A film of the occasion was made by the Ministry of Public Information and shown in all the larger theaters of Korea for a week. An Associated Press dispatch carried the story throughout the United States and Canada.

This was the crowning moment of my life, all the more gratifying because it had taken me thirty-five years to achieve it; all the more gratifying because it had seemed so impossible so many times along the way; all the more gratifying because I *had* managed to change the look on the face of one more Korean boy, and more than one.

The next afternoon, when the boys had gone into the fields to work, I strolled into one of the classrooms. I wanted to enjoy the school for a few minutes of quiet and to think over all that had happened to me.

Outside, two of my boys were working hard and yet effortlessly with their lithe animal grace. One wielded a shovel and one attacked the newly upturned clods with a hoe. I thought to myself, "Is there any more wonderful sight than to see a youth out of doors, busy at work in which he takes pride—healthy, independent, and free!"

And my pleasure was increased when there came to my mind the picture I had seen so often on my travels to the villages—the men of my country standing patiently in line, the empty A-frames on their backs, hoping for one hour's work, for something that would enable them to bring a little food home to their families. No, *my* boys would not be like that. They would be trained. They would be ready to fill a need, to serve their country.

I thought of them coming from the fields, faces flushed, muscles weary, but minds eager and alert, turning to their books at night, to their teachers during the day, questioning, always questioning:

"How did that happen? What makes it run? Why is that so? Why? Why? Why?"

The head, the heart, and the hand. That is the ideal of education.

Yes, no doubt of it, yesterday was the crowning moment of my life; I sighed happily because I had received in full measure the fruits of thirty-five years of struggle.

But for me, it was not so much a happy ending, as it was a joyous beginning. The dreamer must keep on dreaming. If I had accomplished all this in the face of obstacles and disappointments, why shouldn't I do much, much more?

I fell to thinking about the future. First, finish the other wing on the building so that the school would no longer look, as I described it to a friend, "like a chicken with its tail cut off."

Next, provide accommodations for sixty boys the following year, and ninety boys the third year, and . . .

See that the boys were thoroughly trained in "agri-business": How much is my land worth? How much is my labor worth? What should I pay for seeds? What should I pay for fertilizer? When should I purchase a tractor? How much can I save by buying through a co-op? When can I expand my acreage and my production?

And after that—research: To find out which are the better seeds, how the soil can be used to best advantage; which strains produce the healthiest animals. In this way farming can become a fulfilling way of life instead of an indeterminate sentence of drudgery.

Then the amenities: music, literature, handicrafts, the arts.

But not too far in the future I can see that the study course must be lengthened to five years, since the boys will need a much more thorough grounding than we can now provide.

Also, not too far away—Induk Vocational Junior College.

Someday we will add a chapel. That has always been a part of my dream. It will be a memorial chapel to commemorate the sacrifice of American boys who lost their lives in the Korean War and also the sacrifices of our own Koreans who, too, lost their lives.

I have in mind just the location for it—one of the most beautiful and appropriate in all Korea. That is on a terrace up above the field from which the hill has been removed. There is room not only for the chapel, but for walks and meditation groves, and commemorative tablets. I hope to have stained glass in that chapel and a powerful pipe organ.

Sometimes I let my imagination soar—and then I see other Bereas springing up all over Korea and beyond our borders throughout Southeast Asia as well.

And why not?

Whittier's prophetic words:

> Each rude and jostling fragment soon
> Its fitting place shall find,—
> The raw material of a state,
> Its muscle and its mind!

are as applicable to our part of the world today as they were to pioneer America a century or so ago when he wrote them.

My glance strayed out of the picture window of the classroom. Now that the hill was gone, the window afforded a perfect view of Yongmauri (Dragon Head Mountain), gray and purple over there in the distance; and also the back of Sitting Buddha Mountain. Yes, a breath-taking view and one conducive to quiet meditation and mellow reflection.

Ah, lucky boys! How I would like to pass the rest of my days right here, with them. I would spend much time sitting and looking out the picture window at that view—a view ever refreshed, ever renewed, ever changing with the passing of the seasons—brown in autumn, white in winter, wearing its lush mantle of green in the summertime. I would be here to watch the school grow and I would love every minute of it.

But alas, that is not my destiny. I will derive my satisfaction from knowing that my daughter Iris will be here on the scene, with her most productive years still ahead of her, running the school, keeping my dream alive.

As for myself, I will soon be back in the States again, riding the sit-up bus from lecture date to lecture date—Canajoharie to Conneaught; Vincennes to Vancouver; Cheyenne to Calgary.

We may meet some night on that bus. You will know me when I say,

"I am Korean. Perhaps you would like me to tell you something about my country."

We will talk for a while, and then I will smile and say goodby, for I am getting off at the next stop.

There is no rest for me—so long as I still have the chance to change the look on the face of one Korean boy.

The Tiger must be forever on the prowl.